LIBRARIANSHIP AND BUREAUCRATIC ORGANISATION

CONCEPTS IN COMMUNICATION INFORMATICS & LIBRARIANSHIP (CICIL)

General Editor: **S.P. AGRAWAL**

CICIL-1 Development of Library Services in India: Social Science Information **S.P. Agrawal** Rs. 150

CICIL-2 Development of Documentation in India: Social Science Information **S.P. Agrawal** Rs. 250

CICIL-3 UNESCO and Social Sciences: Retrospect and Prospect **S.P. Agrawal** and **J.C. Aggarwal** Rs. 250

CICIL-4 INDIANA: A Bibliography of Bibliographical Sources **M.K. Jain** Rs. 200

CICIL-5 Dimensions of Library and Information Science: Papers contributed in honour of the 61st birthday celebrations of Prof. P.N. Kaula **V. Venkatappaiah** (Ed.) Rs. 600

CICIL-6 Book Numbers: Some Indian Methods **M.P. Satija** and **S.P. Agrawal** Rs. 100

CICIL-7 National Policy for University Libraries in India: Problems and Perspectives **N.B. Inamdar** and **L.S. Ramaiah** (Ed.) Rs. 250

CICIL-8 Media Utilisation for the Development of Women and Children **B.S. Thakur** and **Binod C. Agrawal** Rs. 150

CICIL-9 Terrorism: An Annotated Bibliography **Susheela Bhan** (Ed.) Rs. 275

CICIL-10 Transnational Library Relations: The Indo-American Experience **M.B. Konnur** Rs. 175

CICIL-11 Geography of Marketing and Commercial Activities in India (Documentation on Research Information) **R.S. Dixit** Rs. 130

CICIL-12 Information India 1988: Global View **S.P. Agrawal** and **J.C. Aggarwal** Rs. 200

CICIL-13 Women's Education in India: Historical Review, Present Status and Perspective Plan **S.P. Agrawal** and **J.C. Aggarwal** (in press)

CICIL-14 Phonogram and Cultural Communication in India **J.M. Ojha** (in press)

CICIL-15 Second Historical Survey of Educational Documents in India: Select Documents 1985-1989 **S.P. Agrawal** and **J.C. Aggarwal** (in press)

CICIL-16 Documentation Encyclopaedia of UNESCO and Education **J.C. Aggarwal** and **S.P. Agrawal** (in press)

CICIL-17 Attitude Towards Information: A Study of Post-Graduate Teachers and Researchers in Social Sciences **N.G. Satish** (in press)

CICIL-18 Librarianship and Bureaucratic Organisation: A Study in the Sociology of Library Profession in India **P.K. Jayaswal** Rs. 175

CICIL-19 Literature Search **K.A. Issac** Rs. 150

CICIL-20 Child Education in India: Index to Scholarly Writings in Indian Educational Journals and Newspapers since Independence **S.P. Agrawal** and **Naresh Kanta** Rs. 100

CICIL-21 Lok Sabha and Vidhan Sabha Elections in India 1989 & 1990: Process and Results with Comparative Study of Manifestos **S.P. Agrawal** and **J.C. Aggarwal** Rs. 250

CICIL-22 Islamic Studies in India: A Survey of Human, Institutional and Documentary Sources **Mohamed Taher** (in press)

CICIL-23 Panchayati Raj: An Annotated Bibliography **N.B. Inamdar** (in press)

CICIL-24 Information India 1989-90: Global View **S.P. Agrawal** and **J.C. Aggarwal** Rs. 500

Concepts in Communication
Informatics & Librarianship-18

General Editor: S.P. AGRAWAL

LIBRARIANSHIP AND BUREAUCRATIC ORGANISATION

A Study in the Sociology of Library Profession in India

P.K. JAYASWAL

CONCEPT PUBLISHING COMPANY, NEW DELHI-110059

ISBN 81-7022-321-0

First Published 1990

Published by
Ashok Kumar Mittal
Concept Publishing Company
A/15-16, Commercial Block, Mohan Garden
NEW DELHI-110059 (India)

Lasertypeset by
Microtech Advance Printing Systems (Pvt.) Ltd.
H-13, Bali Nagar
NEW DELHI-110015

Printed in India by
Taj Press
DELHI-110006

GENERAL EDITOR'S INTRODUCTION

DR. P.K. JAYASWAL, who had all along been a student of Sociology, especially in his post-graduate educational career, in this revised version of his work has investigated an important area and aspect of librarianship.

If a librarian were to appraise and rate himself, will there be a distortion by way of self-dramatisation; is a longer-than-life image likely to emerge?

Lack of avenues for progress affects morale and mobility of those at the lower rung. Introduction of running scales can help ameliorate feeling of stagnation. Migration is another way out, while 'Go West' slogan has attracted some, a few have gone 'down under' to go up the ladder, in terms of monetary returns and/or for designations.

In recent days, a concerted campaign has been launched to fill posts with Scheduled Caste/Scheduled Tribe candidates. The profession herein was limited to Hindus. We are now witness to a social phenomenon of more and more groups wanting to stand up and be counted under SC/ST or Backward Class categories.

If the motivation to choose a career in librarianship is not strong, and if it is not to be just a "last refuge", changes in different areas are called for.

How will the profession get infusion of new blood? Will it be in sufficient quality? What will be its quality? These are some of the questions to which the 'professional organisations' would do well to address themselves.

S.P. AGRAWAL

GENERAL EDITOR'S INTRODUCTION

PREFACE

SOCIOLOGICAL STUDIES on professions in India is of very late origin. Some significant works in this field started appearing only after the seventies. These studies covered primarily the medical, legal and academic professions. A few empirical studies were also carried out on engineers, scientists, managers and journalists. But there is hardly any significant work on librarians in India.

Libraries existed in India, in some form or other, from ancient to colonial periods. But it was only after Independence that conscious attempts have been made to establish libraries, as organisations, for educational, social and scientific purposes. The proliferation of knowledge and development of print and non-print media have brought tremendous changes in the structure and functions of libraries. As a result, more and more professionally trained librarians are needed to organise the libraries on scientific and professional basis. Libraries, now, have become complex organisations. The quality of work-force in libraries have also undergone a great change. The process of change in library organisations has, thus, brought complexities in role structures of librarians.

Inquiry into the consequences of bureaucratisation of profession has become one of the important considerations in the study of professions. With the changed 'work ecology' of professionals, both full-fledged professions and semi-professions have become organisation based. Bureaucratisation and professionalisation are thus, inevitable processes for the organisational professionals. But there would be varying consequences of bureaucratisation for each type of professionals, depending upon their degree of professionalisation and work-milieu. The present work is unique in respect of investigating the elements of bureaucratisation and professionalisation in varying organisational contexts in which librarians in Indian libraries perform their roles.

The present work is the revised version of the thesis entitled *Professionals in Organisations: A Study of Trained Librarians in University, Public and Special Libraries*, submitted to the Jawaharlal Nehru University (Centre for the Study of Social Systems) New Delhi.

The study has been presented in ten chapters.

The problem of the study, has been discussed in Chapter One. In order to investigate the professional librarians in terms of their professional characteristics, socio-economic base, occupational careers and roles, it is considered necessary to examine the various approaches concerning these above aspects. Therefore, characteristics of professions have been discussed; inter-relationship between professionalisation and bureaucratisation have been shown; the close relationship between profession and social structure has been established and the importance of careers and roles for the study of occupations has been emphasised.

The design of the study; the universe, the sample tools and techniques have been presented in Chapter Two.

Chapter Three briefly traces the development of library profession in India.

Chapter Four mainly explores the socio-economic background of librarians. The professionals have been examined in detail in terms of sex-differentials, age-structure, marital status, religion, caste, linguistic-regional background, rural-urban background, family background, economic status, educational and professional attainments and organisational attributes.

The occupational career of librarians has been studied in Chapter Five. For the comprehensive study of occupational career, the following aspects have been covered:

(a) the motivational orientations for the choice of occupation;
(b) the sources of communication for occupational choice;
(c) career mobility;
(d) occupational prestige and
(e) occupational satisfaction.

The study of various dimensions of role has been covered in three chapters. Chapter Six presents the role commitment, role perception and role obligation of librarians. Their role-images and value orientations have been explored in Chapter Seven. The framework of role relations has been reported in Chapter Eight. The types of role relations discussed in this chapter include: super-subordinate relations, colleaguial relations and professional-client relations.

Chapter Nine intends to examine the degree of bureaucratisation and professionalisation as perceived by librarians in course of their role performance and Chapter Ten covers the major findings of the study.

ACKNOWLEDGEMENTS

I AM most grateful to Professor T.K. Oommen under whose guidance and supervision the above research work was conducted. He provided continuous encouragement and intellectual stimulus which made it possible for me to complete this work. He was also instrumental in inducting me into M. Phil course at the Centre for the Study of Social Systems, School of Social Sciences, Jawaharlal Nehru University, New Delhi.

I am immensely obliged to Shri Girja Kumar, former Librarian and Shri V.B. Nanda, present Librarian of the Jawaharlal Nehru University who provided me with the opportunity for availing study leave to complete the field-work. The existence of the present work could not be envisaged without their institutional and professional support. I am also thankful to the other authorities of the University and to my colleagues of the Jawaharlal Nehru University Library for their kind cooperation in this regard.

I am also obliged to the Indian Council of Social Science Research for financial assistance for the processing of the field data; and the Director, Data Archives, ICSSR, for extending their guidance and help in statistical treatment of the data.

I have benefited largely from the discussions and consultations at various stages of my work with Shri Girja Kumar, Dr. J.S. Gandhi, Dr. Karuna Chanana, Prof. Kuldeep Mathur, Dr. P.C. Jain, Dr. Lakhan Singh, Dr. M.C. Paul, Shri A.K. Gupta, Shri R. Goswami and Shri C.V. Subba Rao. I am thankful to Prof. P.B. Mangla, Late Prof. T.S. Rajagopalan, Prof. T.N. Rajan, Shri C.P. Vashisht, Shri H.C. Jain and Prof. G.K. Chadha, who were anxious to see the work completed. I express my gratitude to them.

It is not a small fortune to have a lengthy questionnaire filled in by so many professionls, which is the foundation of the work. I owe a great deal to them on that account. I also express my thanks to the staff of National Institute of Health and Family Welfare Library, Nehru Memorial Museum and Library, National Science Library, National Social Science Documentation Centre and Jawaharlal Nehru University Library who provided me with the necessary facilities in the course of my research work.

I record my full appreciation to my wife Smt. Chandrawati and my daughters Priti, Priya and Prachi who helped me in the complete process by sharing most of the family responsibilities ungrudingly and patiently.

I am thankful to Ms. Kunjamme Varghese for typing the final manuscript and Shri M.S. Patwardhan for his kind help rendered in the revision of the manuscript for publication.

I am specially thankful to Dr. S.P. Agrawal, former Director, National Social Science Documentation Centre and the General Editor of the *CICIL* for including my work in the Series.

My sincere thanks are due to Mr. Ashok Kumar Mittal of M/s Concept Publishing Company, New Delhi, for his meticulous and qualitative production of the present work in the book form.

Deputy Librarian
Jawaharlal Nehru University
New Delhi-110067.

P.K. JAYASWAL

CONTENTS

LIST OF TABLES

ONE

INTRODUCTION

THE PROCESS of industrialisation brought many significant changes in the occupational order during nineteenth century. Changes in the occupational situations were so diversified that it was felt that the same process might lead to the disintegration of the concept of profession.[1] Doubts were even raised whether the traditional professions as characterised by their intense individualism would be able to fulfil their appropriate roles in the society. Some viewed professions as being unsympathetic or indifferent to social planning.[2] In contrast, others found that professions were being weaned from excessive individualism and were adopting themselves to the new standards of social service.[3] As a consequence of changes, professionals were able to break their traditional isolation and were ready to work as a team. Thus, professions began getting socialised and the social and public services professionalised. As Goode put it, "an industrializing society is a professionalizing society".[4]

An ideal-typical image of a professional who considered himself as a master of his own, having his own resources for carrying out his work, possessing specialised knowledge and an influential personality was greatly affected by the process of change.[5] A trend was evident among these independent practitioners to shift their work to organisations. The independent practitioners, as a result of their changed work-milieu, were being gradually transformed into a new breed of professional employees, possessing somewhat different set of characteristics. The process of transformation was accelerated by various factors, some of those which draw our attention are: the growth of specialised knowledge, the increasing division of labour, the need for capital investment and the increasing responsibility of the state to provide public service.[6] Under the new situation, it was rather impossible for a "Solo practitioner" to work in isolation. Thus, organisations became a necessity for professional activities. Besides established professions, work-milieu for marginal and other new professions were also becoming essentially organisation based.

Given the changed work-ecology of professionals, it was predicted that "the status and style of functioning of professionals are likely to be moulded by the nature of public policy of state in which they function".[7] The consequences of governmentalisation and/or bureaucratisation of professions have largely drawn the attention of the sociologists. The methodological assumptions underlying such studies were based on the traditional concepts of professions and organisations as two separate systems or institutions.[8] While inescapability of the organisation for occupational existence was well-recognised, still two 'models' — professional and bureaucratic — were used for analysing the supposed "two worlds". Though profession and organisation share certain common characteristics such as universal standard, specific expertise, affective neutrality, they are contrasted on certain different principles. The profession has been characterised as 'an autonomous community of shared interest' and organisation represents a 'rational structure' which must be insulated from its surroundings institutional environment. The contrast is drawn between the vertical structure of the organisation and the horizontal structure of the profession.[9] The source of control of professionals stems from colleaguial authority and in an organisation it is based on hierarchical system of authority. Apparently both these systems rest on fundamentally different principles. Therefore, consequences or dilemmas faced by professionals participating in two irreconcilable systems of profession and bureaucracies were considered significant areas for investigation. Consequently a large number of authors had examined the specific problems of role — incongruity, role strain and professional behaviour as modified or affected in an organisational setting.[10]

Since our primary objective is to analyse the consequences of professionals working in organisations, it is necessary for us to know the crucial attributes of profession. It would enable us to identify those attributes which are most likely to be affected by organisational environment.

CHARACTERISTICS OF A PROFESSION

In social sciences, there is generally a lack of consensus on definitions, and the concept of profession is not an exception. Most of the definitions of professions overlap in the elements, traits or attributes. Sociological writings in the area of professions are mainly concerned with the problem of distinguishing a profession from a non-profession and the process of professionalisation.[11] An analysis of such writings indicates that there are some crucial attributes of a profession. Though variation exists in the nature of attributes as identified by several authors, it is possible to sort out some most common attributes which are: (a) generalised knowledge; (b) primary orientation to the common interest; (c) internalised code of ethics and (d) rewards which primarily symbolise work attainment.[12]

The first attempt to define a profession was made by Flexner.[13] The distinctive trait of a professional, according to him, is an altruistic orientation. Carr-Saunders and Wilson gave emphasis on the presence of an intellectual technique, acquired by special training.[14] As the term intellectual training was 'found incompatible to Parsons, he suggested that a professional knowledge can be gathered in and transmitted to the form of scientific discipline or can be applied in the form of service.[15] But it may be mentioned here that Parsons' approach to profession was more theoretically oriented based on his distinction between *universalistic* (modern) *particularistic* (traditional) societies, rather than simple descriptions of characteristics of profession. According to him, profession as well as business are characterised by *rationality, functional specificty, and universalism* derived from the fundamental character of modern societies.[16]

Further insights into the professional characteristics have been provided by Gross.[17] He gave stress on professional involvement and professional identification. A professional is characterised by a high level of involvement in dealing with clients. He also maintains a close relationship with his colleagues through formal and informal professional associations. The above two characteristics combined together provide him the professional authority and control over the clients.

Some additional criteria, suggested by Goode, also draw our attention in this regard.[18] One of such criteria is the system of prolonged training for acquiring substantive body of knowledge. Through the mechanism of formal training, appropriate professional attitude and behaviour are inculcated among the new members. And as a result of such socialisation process, members become incapable of changing occupations. Another significant characteristic which Goode pointed out, is the power dimension of the profession. Profession is regarded as a powerful force in the society. Hughes brought out the concept of professionalisation. Professionalisation, according to him, is "a change of status of the occupation in relation to its own past and in its work sphere."[19] For the evaluation of a profession, Turner and Hodge present four facets of professionalisation: (a) the degree of substantive theory and practice; (b) the degree of monopoly over particular service; (c) the degree of external recognition and; (d) the degree of organisation of a profession.[20] Thus, the chief characteristics of a profession, according to them, are: autonomy, monopoly and authority. They view profession as a set of role relationship between professional and the client. There are two key factors in the professional/client relationship: (a) autonomy of the professional in work setting, and (b) trust of the client that the professional is working in clients, best interest.[21] To ensure the monopoly of a profession, the professional builds up a veil of mystification around old practices. He also attempts to strengthen its practices by introducing new and complex ideas into it. By this mechanism, a profession gets autonomy and power in the society. So centrality of power is considered as key variable for the study of professions.

PROFESSIONALS IN ORGANISATIONS

As hinted above, our main concern is to understand consequences of professions and professionals when they get situated in organisations. It is not to be assumed that all the attributes of a profession may be equally affected by the impact of organisations. Therefore, it would be worthwhile to identify those attributes which are likely to be affected and others which are likely to remain intact or get adapted. Investigations have shown that most frequently affected attributes are: professional autonomy, service ideals, utilisation of professional knowledge, professional behaviour and attitudes. Among these traits, professional autonomy can be considered as the most critical component of professionalisation.[22] If an organisation does not allow the exercise of autonomy then an individual professional or group cannot utilise their professional abilities. The negative consequences of these attributes usually generate conflicts among professionals working in organisations. The areas of conflicts have been extensively analysed in the relationship between bureaucratisation and professionalisation.

Scott has conceptualised four specific areas which generate conflict: (a) the professional's resistance to bureaucratic rules; (b) the professional's rejection of bureaucratic standards; (c) the professional's resistance to bureaucratic supervision and (d) the professional's conditional loyalty to the bureaucracy.[23] Besides Scott, many others have also emphasised inherent conflicts or contradictions between bureaucratic organisations and professional.[24] To illustrate a few, Dalton suggests that conflicts arise due to incompatibility of bureaucratic and professional authority that hinder goal attainment.[25] Merton finds that adherence to rules in the bureaucratic organisation leads to the displacement of goals of professionals.[26] Daniels also observes that independent initiative and professional judgement is severely limited by the organisation.[27]

Although conflict occurs whenever a professional is employed in an organisation, there is no reason to assume that he will inevitably face conflict. Hall's finding has clearly indicated that it is not necessarily true that the greater the degree of bureaucratisation, the greater the conflict for the professional.[28] Gross has also found that conflict is not inevitable.[29] Similarly there are other researchers who do not regard bureaucracy as completely harmful to the profession. On the contrary, they consider them to be interdependent. For example, Litwak,[30] Smigel[31] and Montagna[32] point to the existence of a new type of organisation which successfully combines the professional and bureaucracy models. Smigel terms such new type of organisation as professional bureaucracy.

Kornhauser, particularly, emphasises that organisations make structural adjustments to mitigate conflicts with professionals.[33] There are evidences which show that both professions and organisations develop adaptive mechanisms and that some role incumbents combine both professional and bureaucratic roles with ease and satisfaction.[34] Therefore, in the final analysis it may be said that although conflicts between profession and bureaucracy may be frequent, but they are not always necessary and eternal.

Blau and Scott[35] and Hall[36] in their studies have clearly suggested that the nature of relationship between profession and bureaucracy depends on how far the professionals are able to control the essential work of organisation. Bucher and Stellings reveal that when professionals control an organisation they eventually create an entirely different kind of organisation which is neither bureaucratic nor professional.[37] It has been suggested that it is not the bureaucratisation *per se* but the degree of professionalisation of occupational group which is likely to affect the organisational structure.[38] Litwak, on the other hand maintains that it is not as much the degree of professionalisation of the occupation as it is the degree of the uniformity of occupational tasks that determines the kind of organisational structure.[39] There is every possibility of professions influencing the very structure of organisations. As such it is appropriate to take into account the different types of settings in which professionals usually work.

Etzioni has recognised three basic types of organisations which employ professionals.[40] (1) In *Professional Organisations*, knowledge is produced, applied, perserved or communicated for specific goals. These organisations are characterised by high proportion of professionals on their staff and they are so structured that professionals have superior authority over the major goal activities of organisations. Based on two distinctive criteria of length of training and authority relation, these organisations may be further divided into two sub-types: (a) "Full-fledged professional" organisations or "Pure" professional organisations are primarily devoted to the creation and application of knowledge. These organisations generally employ professionals who have longer training. Professionals in such organisations are generally protected in their work by the guarantee of priviledged communication. (b) "Semi-professional" organisations are primarily concerned with the communication of knowledge. These organisations employ professionals having shorter training and professionals working in such organisations are likely to be guaranteed the right of privileged communication. In the latter type of organisations, professional work has less autonomy and it is more controlled by those higher in ranks and less subject to the discretion than in full-fledged professional organisations. (2) In *Service Organisations*, professionals are provided with necessary facilities for carrying out their work without being employed or subordinated to their administrative machinery. (3) *Non-Professional Organisations* such as industrial and military establishments also employ professionals who are assigned to carry out specific tasks. Like Etzioni, Scott has also suggested a typology of professional organisations.[41] He considers those organisations as professionals "in which members of one or more professional groups play the central role in the achievement of the primary professional objectives". He identifies *three basic* settings of professional organisations: *autonomous, heteronomous* and *professional department*.

The first type of professional organisation is called *autonomous organisation* in which members of the profession have greater responsibility in defining and implementing the goals of the organisation, setting performance standards and evaluating the standards for their maintenance. In such organisations individual professionals are expected to be highly skilled and motivated and are governed by their internalised professional norms. There is usually a sharp dividing line between professionals and administrative tasks and usually the administrative heads have little jurisdiction over professional work. The distinction between these two types of tasks is always maintained even if the organisation is headed by the professional experts.

As opposed to autonomous organisation, in *heteronomous* setting, *professional employees* are required to work in a subordinated structure and the amount of autonomy usually granted to them is also relatively small. Professionals are controlled by a set of elaborate rules and their tasks are closely supervised by the persons higher in the ranks. The above typology is based on the amount of autonomy granted to professionals by the administrative structure. The degree of professional autonomy is low in the heteronomous organisations.

The third type of setting suggested by Scott is the *professional department*. In this setting, the professional and his department form part of a larger organisation. It is the type of organisation which is often assumed to generate more conflicts for the professionals due to the contradictory situations produced by bureaucratic and professional norms.

While the two typologies are quite useful in understanding the nature of professional organisations, very few specific organisations exactly conform to the "Pure Form". Following Scott's typology, libraries may be characterised as heteronomous organisations. But libraries of universities, colleges, schools or research institutions, may be categorised as professional departments. A big national library of a country or some large special libraries of national level may seem to be more close to autonomous professional organisations. This shows that librarians as professionals can and do exist in three different organisational settings.

It is evident now that work-milieu of both full-fledged professions and semi-professions is essentially organisation based. Barring some of the full-fledged professions, like medicine, law, accountancy, etc. which can be practised either privately or in organisations, there are full-fledged professions, like university teaching which can always be practised in organisations. In the case of semi-professions we find that these are invariably practised in organisations. Librarianship, like nursing, teaching, or social work also falls in the category of semi-professions which are invariably organisation based.

LIBRARIANS AS ORGANISATIONAL PROFESSIONALS

For the study of professionals in organisations, the distinction between full-fledged and semi-professions is important. It may be argued that some of the consequences which have been conceptualised for the full-fledged professionals may not be theoretically valid for majority of semi-professionals which are essentially organisational professionals. It may be further stressed that there would be varying consequences for each type of professionals depending upon their degree of professionalisation and work-milieu. Therefore, there is need to examine a specific category of profession in its organisational context. The present work looks at trained librarians working in different settings of Indian libraries, to investigate the elements of professionalisation and bureaucratisation and their inter-relations.

PROFESSIONS AND SOCIAL STRUCTURE

Occupations are a major link between society and the individual. They serve as a source of placements of individuals or groups in the social life. According to Hughes "Professions provide a channel of mobility not simply to individuals but for entire groups — ethnic, caste and religious".[42]

The knowledge of occupational structure enables us to understand the social system. The specific characteristics of occupations are reflected in the social structure. In this context, Blau and Duncan rightly mention that, "in the absence of hereditary castes or feudal estates, class differences came to rest primarily in occupational positions and the economic advantages and powers are associated with them".[43] The close association between occupations and social status led may scholars to study social stratification by studying occupational stratification.

The studies of occupations have consistently shown that the older professions are still accorded the highest status and the members of some professions are highly privileged group in modern society. Of several studies, the first which focuses our attention on the prestige dimension is by Davis and Moore.[44] They suggest that greater prestige rewards are allocated to occupations on the basis of their functional importance in a society. It means that certain professions which are functionally more important in a society, would be accorded higher rewards. Moreover, it has also been seen that functionally important occupations are those that: (a) demand larger training, (b) greater sacrifices and (c) larger period of education. They observe that since workers in high status professions tend to be scarce so a system of awards is necessary to recruit people in it. Thus, in order to answer ". . . as to why different positions carry different degree of prestige . . . and . . . how certain individuals get into those position,[45] Davis and Moore clearly specify two factors which are: (a) differential functional importance of the profession and (b) differential scarcity of personnel.[46] The latter factor is ultimately related to the "means" available to individuals or "groups" for entry into the profession.

Needless to say that these factors which determine the status of occupation would be affected differently by the differences in stratification system. Occupations important in one society may not be important in another because of the differences in the degrees of internal development of these societies. The position taken by Davis and Moore was also supported by Froomkin and Jaffe who mentioned that the level or skill assigned to a particular occupation is a function of the particular socio-economic conditions of the country.[47]

In their study of classification of occupations in the United States and the Soviet Union, Froomkin and Jaffe found that many jobs classified as skilled in the Soviet Union in 1926 were classified as semi-skilled in American society of 1950.[48] Apparently it would imply that if a job skill would become more common, it would require less training, and as it would be conceived less important, so it would be awarded less money and prestige. Hatt and North similarly contended that "highly specialised training and a considerable degree of responsibility for the public services appeared to be the chief factors moving for job prestige".[49]

Thus, it is evident that an enquiry into the status of occupations would require not only the knowledge of social structure but also how new members are recruited in the profession and how the process of recruitment is controlled or monopolised by a particular group of people. The factor which greatly affects the status of the profession is the amount of education or training required. In general, the more stringent the entrance requirements, the higher the status of the occupations. Etzioni's classification of professions clearly indicates that "the members of full-fledged professions" require greater length of training and education while those in semi-professions, less so.[50]

This would imply that entry into full-fledged profession is restricted to those group of persons who can afford to have high amount of education. But the high investment in education is commensurate with economic power. Tumin[51] and Lenski[52] correctly assess that parental position and power play a dominant role in educational and eventually occupational attainments. Studies in the area of process of recruitment into professional occupations clearly demonstrate that occupations have been and still are self-recruited or recruited from a particular class or status group within a society.[53]

Viewed against this background, especially relating to the factors suggested by Davis and Moore, it may be stated that since the importance given to the role of librarianship, or the status accorded to the profession is likely to differ greatly in industrialised advanced societies and traditional developing societies, it would be fruitful to study the status of librarianship as a profession in a developing society like India.

OCCUPATIONAL CAREER

The concept of career is particularly relevant to profession. It is applicable to both types of professionals – independent practitioners and professional employees. In the broad sense, occupational career serves as the major source for the stability of the society.[54] Its study reveals the structure of the occupation and the place of individual within it. The concept is useful in understanding and analysing the dynamics of work organisations. From the individual's point of view, Hughes defines career as "the moving perspective in which the person sees his life as a whole and interprets the meaning of his various attributes, actions and things which happen to him.[55]

According to the above perspective, as suggested by Hughes, career refers to a "series of status", "sequences of positions", and patterned series of adjustment made by the individual to the 'network of institutions, formal organisations and informal relationships".[56] The orderly movement from one job to another may be referred to as career pattern. Wilensky defines career pattern as "a succession of related jobs, arranged in a hierarchy of prestige, through which persons move in an ordered, predictable sequence".[57] Occupations are characterised by typical and orderly career patterns, while individuals in them have careers, which, in most cases, are disorderly. Let us take the case of a professional librarian in an Indian university library who usually has four career steps open to him: Professional Assistant, Assistant Librarian, Deputy Librarian and Librarian. While many individuals proceed in an orderly manner through these steps, a few may have more disorderly careers in librarianship. An individual may be a professional assistant in a university library, move to a college for a temporary post of an assistant professor, may come back to the university as assistant librarian, may move further as associate professor in the university and so forth. However, such individual variation and disorder does not lead to conclude that an orderly pattern is not associated with the occupation. Wilensky also feels, that career should refer to the vertical mobility, but sociologically it refers to any pattern of occupational change vertical and/or horizontal of any occupational group.[58]

The horizontal aspect of career movement has been highly emphasised by Becker in his study of 'The Career of the Chicago Public School Teacher'.[59] He contends that it need not be assumed that occupational positions which share some characteristics because of their similar rank in a formal structure are identical in all aspects. His study demonstrates that the entire career of school teachers can be characterised as movements at one level of work hierarchy in search of most satisfactory work place. Elliot also supports this notion by pointing out that different practice situations, although formally at the same level within a hierarchy, may be accorded very different prestige and status within the profession.[60]

Slocum[61] makes distinction between career mobility and occupational mobility. While the former describes career development within occupations the latter describes movement between occupations. He writes "career mobility involves moving from one occupational stage to another. This may involve promotion to a more responsible position, demotion, discharge, moving to another organisation or retirement".[62]

Based on the studies of careers in various occupations, some authors have suggested the different steps or stages and strategies in career pattern. Miller and Form have recognised five general steps for all career patterns. The phases of a career are: (a) Preparatory period; (b) Initial period; (c) Trial period; (d) Stable period and (e) Retirement. The first two phases are concerned with socialisation of individuals for occupational system. In the fourth stage an individual develops a strong commitment to his occupational position which continues until retirement or another change in the job.[63]

It may be said that the above steps of career patterns are not only useful for analysing information about career but also provide an insight into the relationship between occupational structure and the mobility of individuals. However, there is likely to be a great deal of individual variation in real situations. Thus, it is helpful to consider them as ideal types.[64]

Thompson *et al.* suggest four strategies of career patterns: (a) Heuristic approach; (b) Occupational strategy; (c) Organisational strategy and (d) Stability strategy.[65] An individual takes heuristic approach when he sacrifices occupational or organisational boundaries and dedicates his efforts only for advancement in the career. In the second strategy, he gives importance to occupation and disregards organisational placements. The person may be considered to be following an organisational strategy when he totally depends upon the employing organisation for opportunities in his career. He ultimately resorts to take stability strategy when he considers all other jobs as irrelevant to him and seeks satisfaction or resignation with the present position.

In the profile of a medical doctor, Hall identifies four stages in the growth of a professional medical practitioner: (a) generating of an occupation; (b) gaining admittance to professional institutions; (c) acquiring a clientele, retaining and improving it and perhaps eventually transferring into a successor and (d) developing a set of informal relationship with colleagues which facilitate the above.[66]

It may be recognised that the above stages would perhaps apply better in the case of a free practitioner than that of a professional employee. In fact there are two distinct situations concerning the career mobility of these two types of professionals. While the career pattern of an independent practitioner is usually governed by the norms of professional organisation, by evaluation of his peers; and also by the generalised clientele community. On the other hand, the career mobility of an organisational professional is largely to be governed by the norms and rules of organisations and his performance is usually measured through some bureaucratic standards laid down by employing organisations beforehand.

Studies concerning the occupational career patterns have shown that even different types of organisational professionals adopt different routes in their careers. Ritzer notes that the professionals are characterised by extreme diverse career patterns due to their long professional preparatory programmes; and semi-professions, on the other hand, offer slightly more career mobility.[67] Becker has also demonstrated that semi-professionals, like teachers, take a good deal of lateral mobility.[68] Wilensky's description about the different work situations permitting different types of career mobility is also important in this respect.[69]

While each occupation has its peculiar role demands and orientations, it is important question to ask why a person embarks upon a particular occupation or career. Studies of occupational choice suggest that the range of alternatives available to an individual for the choice of his career is very limited and narrow.[70] The individual is restricted by the limited information available to him and the importance of social milieu in which his identity is established. While the deliberate or conscious choice for a career may likely to increase his role commitment and satisfaction, his accidental entry to the occupation may lead also to random job mobility and occupational frustration or resignation. It is not always correct to think that careers can only advance:

> Occupational careers (like illness careers) can and do suffer setbacks, resulting in loss of status, prestige or pay. Yet the term career is generally reserved for those occupations which provide for formal advance skill, status or rewards.[71]

Against the above backdrop, it is one of our main aims to investigate the occupational career of librarians in terms of their motivational orientations for choosing the librarianship as a career; the extent of satisfaction or prestige which librarianship bestows on them and the sources of mobility which they experience in their careers.

CONCEPT OF ROLE

The concept of role has assumed key positions in cultural anthropology, social psychology and sociology. Its complete history has been provided by Thomas and Biddle.[72] Invariably all social scientists acknowledge their debt to Ralph Linton for the concept of role.[73] As an anthropologist, Linton was interested in cultural patterns. For him, role is "the sum total of the ideal patterns which control the reciprocal behaviour between individual and the society.[74] Parsons used the concept of role in context of his general theory of social action.[75] His definition of role includes actor's orientation to situations. Several psychologists give emphasis on the individual perceptions of roles. Some role analysts equate role with the actual behaviour of the actors occupying social positions.[76] Goffman makes distinction between three types of role: typical role, the normative aspect of role and the actual performance of role; and he also defines role as "the typical response of individuals in a particular position".[77]

The concept of role has thus been used by several authors for analysing different problems. In the study of occupations, the concept has also assumed a dominant position. It is through roles that tasks are allocated in the society. Soloman contends that much of occupational sociology can be understood in terms of role theory:

> Once an occupational level identifies a category of persons it is implied that they behave or can legitimately be expected to behave in the same or similar ways in given situations, that they have similar roles to perform. . . . An occupation can be thought of as a role. . . .[78]

The concept of role has been found very useful in examining the interface between professionals and organisation. Hickson maintains that role theory may be the key to understanding the various perspectives of organisations.[79] When professionals work in organisations, it is their roles which are likely to be affected by organisational norms. For many occupations, the role of the employees is defined by the employing organisation. In case of professions, the definition of role lies with the professionals as prescribed by their associations.

The concept has been used for analysing varieties of problems. Despite this, the concept is still considered as "vague, nebulous and non-definitive" and "it remains one of the most over worked and underdeveloped in social sciences".[80] There is also a great deal of semantic confusion about the concept. Oommen contends that much of the inadequacies of the concept emanate from the fact that role is a nominal concept, unsuited to be used for generating propositions.[81] For application of the concept, he suggests that one should first dimensionalise it in terms of certain variables and then operationalise these variables in order to measure their degree or direction.

Following the same line of approach, we intend to dimensionalise the concept of role in terms of *perception*, *obligation*, *relation*, *interaction*, *commitment* etc. and then operationalise these variables in order to measure the direction of role perception; the degree of role commitment; the content of relation or interaction etc. in the case of trained librarians.

ROLE COMMITMENT

The term 'commitment' is often used in the context of role. When an individual regularly performs his role, he is more or less committed to it. It means that the individual has identified himself with a particular behaviour. Having identified with a role, he must find mechanisms to sustain it. Thus 'consistent line of activity' may be termed as commitment. The notion of commitment, according to Becker implies that the individual has chosen one feasible alternative out of several alternative courses.[82] The person, when he makes 'side bets' is also constrained to his future activity. He thus becomes "locked into a position and coerced into living up to the promises and sacrifices built into it".[83] Becker observes that:

> If a person refuses to change jobs even though the new job would offer him a higher salary and better working conditions, we should suspect that his decision is a result of commitment, that other sets of rewards than income and working conditions have become attached to his present job so that it would be painful for him to change. He may have a large pension at stake, which he will loss if he moves; he may dread few cost of making new friends and learning to get along with new working associates; he may feel that he will get a reputation for living flightly and erratic if leaves the present job. In each instance, formerly extraneous interests have become linked to his present job.[84]

Undoubtedly organisation plays an important role in shaping the role commitment of individuals. When the organisation provides the opportunities for using professional knowledge and abilities, the employees would apparently depend upon it and their commitment to occupational tasks would increase. But when the organisation is not dependable or fails to provide with meaningful tasks, the commitment of individuals would diminish.[85]

One might predict that a professional group in any organisation would be more committed to professional roles than any other groups. It is expected that they would maintain closer ties with professional organisations and colleagues and strive for increasing intellectual or professional content in their roles. The assumption is based on the process of role training which a professional undergoes for initiation into an occupation. On the other hand, low degree of occupational commitment may be the consequences of weak pre-entry motivation or lack of internalisation of professional norms in occupational training. Oommen contends that "the possibility of 'weak' pre-entry motivation, getting transformed into 'strong' occupational commitment through appropriate occupational socialisation and adequate reward mechanisms cannot be ruled out".[86] Keeping this consideration in view the content and degree of role commitment of librarians will be enquired into.

ROLE PERCEPTION

The basic function of any service organisation is to serve clients. The crucial problems of the professionals working in such organisations centre around providing professional services. The welfare of the clients in presumed to be the chief concern of professional personnel. But actually, some basic features of organisations erode service norms, and professionals or semi-professionals most often seem to lose sight of the welfare of the clients. It is either because of their concern with their status and careers or due to pre-occupation with administrative problems.[87] The latter may become manifest in rigid adherence to and enforcement of procedures which may go contrary to the clients' interest. Failure to serve the needs of the clients adequately is a more prevalent problem of service organisations, and libraries probably are no exception.

Not only the professionals become insensitive to the needs of the clients, but sensitivity to the clients often becomes disadvantageous to them.[88] Since client service is of little consequence in matter of promotion or career advancement, professionals become more concerned with gaining approvals of administrative superiors inside the organisation. Contrary to independent professional, the role performance of a professional working in an organisation in judged on the basis of fixed administrative principles, so one tends to be more organisation-oriented rather than client-oriented.

The excessive bureaucratisation of role orientation of professionals usually create problems in identification of their roles with professional groups. Bureaucratic role orientation of professionals is likely to undermine the necessity of developing their professional knowledge and skill or strengthening professional ideology. Consequently they may not need the support of their professional colleagues inside or outside the organisation. In the case of trained librarians, these above trends are likely to influence their role perceptions.

ROLE IMAGES

For a meaningful study of role, it will also be important to have a look at self-role images of librarians and their organisational-role images along with the part played by value orientations in them. A comparison between these two images would indicate the extent of discrepancy between them.

ROLE RELATIONS

Role cannot be studied in isolation, it has to be understood in relation to 'role-others' or 'significant-others'. An incumbent of a position enacts his role in a situation with role-others. The various kinds of role-others, if taken together, or an array of associated roles has been termed by Merton as role-set.[89] A role-set, according to him, would mean "the compliment of role relationships which persons have by virtue of occupying a particular social status".[90] In the context of libraries, we may envisage the following kinds of role–others for librarians, such as (a) superiors and subordinates; (b) colleagues; and (c) clients.

HIERARCHICAL AND COLLEAGUIAL RELATIONS

Studies in the field of formal organisations emphasise two facets of relationships – the impersonal relations between professionals belonging to hierarchical levels and informal relations among professional colleagues in the same organisational level.[91] Distinguishing between two types of authority, formal and informal, Blau and Scott maintain that although formal authority is important for meeting the minimum requirements of operations in a complex organisation, it is not sufficient for attaining efficiency in work-organisation.[92] It has been found that subordinates usually assume more responsibility if they are governed by informal authority. If professionals in organisations would excessively depend upon their formal status for source of power or authority, they are less likely to be strong in social bonds with their colleagues.[93] In sociological theory, the need for strong social ties with colleagues has been greatly stressed. For example, Gross has characterised colleague relationship as *'espirit de crops'* and 'a sense of being in the same boat'.[94] The conception of colleagueship stresses occupational unity. In the context of libraries, it would be an interesting aspect to study as to what type of relations – '*informal-equalitarian*' and/or '*bureaucratic-authoritarian*' — librarians perceive with their professional superiors and peers.[95]

PROFESSIONAL-CLIENT RELATIONSHIP

The client constitutes an important aspect of the role-set for all professionals. The professional-client relationship is the kernal role of the professionals. The characteristics of professional-client relationship have been discussed by several authors.[96] The traditional form or idealised image of professional-client relationship indicates that it is the professional who decides the needs of the clients and provides the expert service or judgement accordingly. The nature of service which professional provides has been characterised by effective neutrality and disinterestedness. The professional supposed to be impersonally detached from the client. The element of detachment insulates the professional so that he may exercise reasoned judgement. Since the professional has the right of privileged communication, he is expected to be loyal to the client. The norms of professional-client relationship is protected by the professional code of ethics. In turn, the client contributes to the professional by paying a fee directly for his services.

There is, however, a growing evidence to suggest that the idealised conception of professional-client relationship does not correspond to reality in many cases. In the case of independent professionals, it is probable that some of the elements of professional-client relation are realised. But, for the organisational professionals it is the employing organisations which arrange clients for them and the nature of client relationship depends upon the practice situations of the organisations. For example, professionals in organisations may deal with the clients either directly (as the doctors in a hospital) or may provide indirect services to them (as in the case of pathologist). Sometimes professionals remain in an ambiguous position in matters of identification of their clients.

The present study investigates the nature of role which librarians assume *vis-a-vis* their clients, and the latter's perception of the former's role. In other words we want to see how far the general pattern of professional-client relationship holds good.

In sum, our objectives in the present study are:

(a) to explore the socio-economic background of librarians;

(b) to examine the motivation for the choice of occupation and to study the career patterns;
(c) to investigate the role images, role-perceptions, role-relations and role-commitments of librarians and
(d) to ascertain the extent of bureaucratisation and professionalisation in terms of some of their key characteristics.

NOTES

1. A.M. Carr-Saunders (1955), "Metropolitan Conditions and Traditional Professional Relationships" in Robert Moore Fisher (ed.), *Metropolis in Modern Life*, New York: Doubleday, pp. 286-87.
2. Harold J. Laski (1935), "The Decline of the Profession", *Harpers' Monthly Magazine*, November, pp. 656-57.
3. T.H. Marshall (1939), "The Recent History of Professionalism in Relation to Social Structure and Social Policy", *The Canadian Journal of Economics and Political Science*, Vol. 5, pp. 337-38.
4. William J. Goode (1960), "Encroachment, Charlatanism and the Emerging Profession: Psychology, Sociology and Medicine", *American Sociological Review*, Vol. 25, pp. 902-14.
5. A.M. Carr-Saunders (1955), op. cit., pp. 286-87.
6. T.K. Oommen (1978), *Doctors and Nurses: A Study of Occupational Role Structure*, Delhi: Macmillan, p. 1.
7. T.K. Oommen (1983), "The Legal Profession in India: Some Sociological Perspectives", *Indian Bar Review*, Vol. 10, pp. 1-46.
8. G. Harries-Jenkins (1970), "Professionals in Organisations", in J.A. Jackson (ed.), *Professions and Professionalisation*, London, Cambridge University Press, p. 53.
9. *Ibid.*, p. 54.
10. *Ibid.*
11. C. Turner and M.N. Hodge (1970), "Occupations and Professions", in J.A. Jackson, op. cit., p. 23.
12. B. Barker (1963), "Some Problems in the Sociology of Professions", *Daedlus*, Vol. 92, pp. 669-88.
13. Abraham Flexner (1915), "Is Social Work a Profession?" in *Proceedings of the National Conference of Charities and Corrections*, Chicago, Hildman, pp. 576-90.
14. A.M. Carr-Saunders and P. A. Wilson (1963), "The Emergence of Professions", in Sigmund Nosow and William H. Form (eds.), *Man, Work and Society*, New York, Basic Books, pp. 199-206.
15. Talcott Parsons (1954), "The Professions and Social Structure", in *Essays in Sociological Theory*, Glencoe, Illinois, Free Press.
16. *Ibid.*
17. Edward Gross (1958), *Work and Society*, New York, Thomas Y. Crowell, pp. 77-82.
18. See especially, William J. Goode (1969), "The Theoretical Limits of

Professionalisation", in Amitai Etzioni (ed.), *The Semi-Professions and Their Organisations: Teachers, Nurses and Social Worker*, New York, Free Press, pp. 266-313; and his another article, "The Librarian: From Occupation to Profession" in Philip H. Ennis and Howard W. Winger (eds.) (1962), *Seven Questions About the Profession of Librarianship*, Chicago, The University of Chicago Press, pp. 8-22.

19. E.C. Hughes (1963), "Professions", *Daedalus* Vol. 92, p. 661.
20. C. Turner and M.N. Hodge (1970), op. cit., p. 26.
21. E.C. Hughes (1963), op. cit., p. 657.
22. Other characteristics such as knowledge base, community sanction, colleague control are considered as elements of autonomy. See, Richard H. Hall (1961), *Occupations and Social Structure*, Englewood Cliffs, New Jersey, Prentice-Hall, p. 81.
23. W. Richard Scott (1966), "Professionals in Bureaucracies: Areas of Conflict", in Howard M. Vollumer and Donald M. Mills (eds.), *Professionalisation*, Englewood Cliffs, Prentice-Hall, pp. 265-75.
24. See especially, Melville Dalton (1954), *Men Who Manage*, New York: John Wiley; M. Aiken and J. Hage (1966), "Organisational, Alienation: A Comparative Analysis", *American Sociological Review*, Vol. 31, pp. 497-507; G.A. Miller (1967), "Professionals in Bureaucracy, Alienation Among Industrial Scientists and Engineers", *American Sociological Review*, Vol. 32, pp. 755-68.
25. Melville Dalton (1950), "Conflicts Between Staff and Line Managerial Officers", *American Sociological Review*, Vol. 15, pp. 342-51.
26. Robert K. Merton (1952), "Bureaucratic Structures and Personality", in *Reader in Bureaucracy*, Glencoe, Ill., Free Press, pp. 361-71.
27. Arlene K. Daniels (1969), "The Captive Professional: Bureaucratic Limitations in the Practice of Military Psychiatry", *Journal of Health and Social Behaviour*, Vol. 10, pp. 255-265.
28. See, Richard H. Hall (1967), "Some Organisational Considerations in the Professional Organisational Relationship" *Administrative Science Quarterly*, Vol. 12, pp. 461-78.
29. M.E.W. Gross (1961), "Influence and Authority Among Physicians in an Outpatient Clinic", *American Sociological Review*, Vol. 26, pp. 39-50.
30. Eugene Litwak (1961), "Models of Bureaucracy which Permit Conflict", *American Journal of Sociology*, Vol. 67, pp. 177-84.
31. Erwin Smigel (1969), *The Wall Street Lawyer*, Bloomington, Indiana University Press.
32. Paul D. Montagna (1968), "Professionalisation and Bureaucratisation in Large Professional Organisation", *American Journal of Sociology*, Vol. 74, pp. 138-45.
33. W. Kornhauser (1962), *Scientists in Industry: Conflict and Accommodation*, Berkeley, University of California Press, p. 8.
34. See Particularly, Leonard Riessman (1949), "A Study of Role Conceptions in Bureaucracy", *Social Forces*, Vol. 27, pp. 305-10; Barney Glaser (1962), "The Local Cosmopolitan Scientists", *American Journal of Sociology*, Vol. 69, pp. 249-59.
35. See Peter M. Blau and W. Richard Scott (1970), *Formal Organisation — A Comparative Approach*, London: Routledge and Kegan Paul, W. Richard Scott, op. cit., pp. 265-75.

36. Richard H. Hall (1968), "Professionalisation and Bureaucratisation", *American Sociological Review*, Vol. 33, pp. 92-103. See also his other article, "Some Organisational Considerations in the Professional Organisational Relationship", op. cit., pp. 461-78.
37. Rue Bucher and Jaon Stellings (1969), "Characteristics of Professional Organisations", *Journal of Health and Social Behaviour*, Vol. 10, pp. 3-15.
38. Richar H. Hall (1968), "Professionalisation and Bureaucratisation", op. cit., p. 103.
39. Eugene Litwak (1961), op. cit., p. 182.
40. Amitai Etzioni (1964), *Modern Organisation*, Englewood Cliff, New Jersey, Prentice-Hall, pp. 77-78.
41. Richard W. Scott (1965), "Reactions to Supervision in a Heteronomous Professional Organisations", *Administrative Science Quarterly*, Vol. 10, pp. 67-81.
42. E.C. Hughes (1960), "The professions in Society", *The Canadian Journal of Economics and Political Science*, Vol. 26, pp. 54-61.
43. Peter M. Blau and Otis Dundley Duncan (1967), *The American Occupational Structure*, New York, John Wiley, p. 8.
44. Kingsley Davis and Wilbert E. Moore (1962), "The Social Allocation of Occupations: A Functional Analysis", in Sigmund Nosow and William H. Form, *Man, Work and Society*, New York, Basic Books, pp. 375-83.
45. *Ibid.*, p. 375.
46. *Ibid.*, p. 377.
47. Joseph Froomkin and A.J. Jaffe (1953), "Occupational Skill and Socio-Economic Structure", *American Journal of Sociology* Vol. 59, pp. 42-48.
48. *Ibid.*
49. Paul K. Hatt and C. C. North (1962), "Prestige Ratings of Occupations", in Sigmund Nosow and William H. Form, op. cit., p. 277.
50. Amitai Etzioni (ed.) (1969), *The Semi-Professions and Their Organisations*, op. cit., p. V.
51. Melvin M. Tumin (1953), "Some Principles of Stratification: A Critical Analysis", *The American Sociological Review*, Vol. 18, pp. 387-95.
52. G. Lenski (1966), *Power and Privilege*, New York: McGraw-Hill, p. 346.
53. A. Saltz (1962), "Occupations Theory and History", in Sigmund Nosow and William H. Form, op. cit., pp. 58-62.
54. Harold J. Wilensky (1962), "Careers, Life Styles and Social Integrations" in Sigmund Nosow and William H. Form, op. cit., p. 329.
55. E.C. Hughes (1958), *Men and Their Work*, Glencoe, Ill., Free Press, p. 63.
56. Oswald Hall (1948), "The Stages of a Medical Career", *American Journal of Sociology*, Vol. 53, p. 327.
57. Harold J. Wilensky (1960), "Work, Careers and Social Integration", *International Social Science Journal*, Vol. 12, p. 554.
58. See Sigmund Nosow and William H. Form (1962), op. cit., p. 284.
59. Howard S. Becker (1971), *Sociological Work: Methods and Substance*, London, Allen Lane, The Penguine Press, pp. 165-176.
60. Philip Elliott (1972), *Sociology of Profession*, London: Macmillan, p. 108.
61. W.C. Solcum (1966), *Occupational Careers*, Chicago, Aldine, 1966, p. 239.
62. *Ibid.*

63. Delbert C. Miller and William H. Form (1951), *Industrial Sociology*, New York, Harper, p. 451; See also, William H. Form and Delbert C. Miller (1962), "Occupational Pattern as a Sociological Instrument", in Sigmund Nosow and William H. Form, op. cit., pp. 287-97.
64. See, George Ritzer (1972), *Man and His Work*, New York: Appleton-Century Crofts, p. 43.
65. James D. Thompson, Robert W. Avery and Richard Garlson (1962), *Occupations, Personnel and Careers*, Pittsburgh, University of Pittsburgh, pp. 12-14.
66. Oswaled Hall (1948), op. cit., pp. 327-336.
67. George Ritzer (1972), op. cit., pp. 44-45.
68. Howard S. Becker (1971), op. cit., pp. 167-76.
69. Harold J. Wilensky (1960), "Careers, Life Styles and Social Integration". op. cit., p. 331.
70. See, M. Rosenberg (1957), et al, *Occupations and Values*, Glencoe, Ill., Free Press, pp. 4-7.
71. Malcolm Johnson (1983), "Professional Careers and Biographies", Robert Dingwall and Philip Lewis (eds.), *The Sociology of the Professions: The Lawyers, Doctors and Others*, London, Macmillan, p. 251.
72. See, Edwin J. Thomas and Bruce J. Biddle (1966), "The Nature and History of Role Theory", in Bruce J. Biddle and Edwin J. Thomas (eds.), *Role Theory: Concepts and Research*, New York: John Wiley, pp. 3-19.
73. Ralph Linton (1936), *The Study of Man*, New York, D. Appleton-Century.
74. *Ibid*., p. 105.
75. Talcott Parsons (1951), *The Social System*, Glencoe, Ill., The Free Press, pp. 38-39.
76. Kingsley Davis (1949), *Human Society*, New York, Macmillan, p. 90.
77. Erving Goffman (1972), *Encounters: Two Studies in the Sociology of Interaction*, London, Allene Lane, The Penguine Press, p. 82.
78. David N. Soloman, "Sociological Perspectives on Occupations", in Howard S. Becker, et al., *Institutions and the Persons*, Chicago, Aldine, 1968, pp. 3-13.
79. David J. Hickson, "A Convergence in Organisational Theory", *Administrative Science Quarterly*, Vol. 11, 1965, p. 225.
80. Lionel J. Neiman and James W. Wughes (1951), "The Problem of the Concept of Role: A Re-survey of the Literature", *Social Forces*, Vol. 30, p. 149.
81. T.K. Oommen, op. cit., pp. 15-16.
82. Howard S. Becker (1960), "Notes on the Concept of Commitment", *American Journal of Sociology*, Vol. 66, pp. 32-42.
83. Irving Goffman (1972), op. cit., p. 78.
84. Howard S. Becker (1964), "Personal Change of Adult Life", *Sociometry*, Vol. 27, pp. 40-53.
85. R.M. Steers (1977), "Antecedents of Outcomes of Organisational Commitment", *Administrative Science Quarterly*, Vol. 22, pp. 46-56.
86. T.K. Oommen (1978), *Doctors and Nurses*, op. cit., p. 18.
87. Peter M. Blau and W. Richard Scott (1970), *Formal Organisations: A comparative Approach*, op. cit., p. 52.
88. Amitai Etzioni (1964), *Modern Organisations*, op. cit., p. 100.
89. Robert K. Merton (1957), *Social Theory and Social Structure* (Rev. ed.), New York, The Free Press, pp. 369-70

90. *Ibid.*, p. 369.
91. Peter M. Blau and W. Richard Scott (1970), op. cit., p. 159.
92. *Ibid.*, pp. 140-59.
93. *Ibid.*
94. Edward Gross (1958), *Work and Society*, New York, Thomas Y. Crowell, pp. 223-35.
95. The categorisation of role relations in terms of informal-equalitarian and bureaucratic-authoritarian has been suggested by, T.K. Oommen, See, *Doctors and Nurses*, op. cit., pp. 164-65.
96. For characteristics of professional-client relationship, see, Amitai Etzioni (ed.), (1964), *The Semi-Professions and their Organisation*, op. cit., pp. 123-30; Howard M. Vollumer and Donald M. Mills (1966), (eds.), *Professionalisation*, op. cit., Chapter 6; and Richard H. Hall (1961), *Occupations and the Social Structure*, op. cit., pp. 130-31.

TWO

METHOD OF STUDY

NATURE OF THE STUDY

LIBRARIANSHIP AS a profession is relatively little studied in India and naturally the body of knowledge available in this area is scanty. There is need to know much more about it. The study was therefore undertaken in the spirit of an exploration to understand the nature and role of professionals working in their organisations.

The objectives required it to be both theoretical and empirical; theoretical inasmuch as the study employs concepts such as profession, bureaucracy, careers, roles etc., and empirical insofar as it seeks to verify the extent of some of these basic or distinguishing characteristics in a sample of librarians. Our purpose is not so much to throw light on the adequacy or otherwise of the existing theories and concepts as it purports to examine the nature of library profession in India at the empirical level. It is hoped that such a diagnosis will elicit practical suggestions for the growth of the profession here.

UNIVERSE OF STUDY

For the purpose of study, Delhi, the capital city of India, was chosen as the universe. As librarians are organisational professionals, it was inevitable to study them in context of their organisations, that is, libraries.

The Union territory of Delhi has the unique distinction of having the largest cluster of libraries and information centres. There are six university libraries in Delhi. The Indian Library Directory[1] lists 11 libraries of national importance, out of which five are located in the city, *viz.* Delhi Public Library, Indian Agricultural Research Institute Library, National Social Science Documentation Centre, National Science Library and the National Medical Library. Being the seat of the Union Government, there are libraries attached to various Ministries, Departments, Commissions and Surveys. Including Government administrative libraries, at present there are 73 other special libraries and information centres attached to research and industrial establishment.[2] The city has nearly 15 per cent of the total libraries of the country.[3]

Besides the numerous well-equipped libraries in the capital, University of Delhi has one of the oldest Departments of Library and Information Science (established in 1947) which imparts professional education up to the highest level. Another institution which provides special training in documentation (INSDOC) is also located in Delhi. The city has enough facilities for para-professional education in the library science. In addition to these, many professional associations of librarians have their headquarters in the city, *viz.*, the Indian Library Association, the Indian Association of Academic Librarians, the Medical Library Association of India, the Association of Government of India Librarians and Information Specialists, Association of Agricultural Librarians and Documentation of India; Society for Information Science and Delhi Library Association.

According to the Government of India Census, 1981,[4] the total number of librarians (including archivists and curators) in India is 21,633. According to the same source there are 2,089 librarians in Delhi.[5] This shows that nearly 10 per cent of the total population of librarians in India are located in Delhi. The Statewise distribution of librarians,[6] presented in Table 2.1, clearly indicates that Delhi has the highest ratio of librarians in relation to its population and ranks highest in respect of women librarians. With more than 70 per cent of libraries established in urban areas librarianship is seen as an urban-based occupation. In the light of these facts, libraries located in Delhi can be said to reflecting the state of Library and Information Science in India.

SELECTION OF LIBRARIES

Classification of libraries is not an easy task and different criteria are used for it. These criteria are: nature of library collection; types of clientele, and functions; pattern of organisation or authority, etc. Libraries are often categorised into three types such as public, academic and special libraries. By public library we mean general libraries catering to the need of public at large. Under the category of academic libraries, we have considered libraries attached to institutions of higher learning and predominantly used by student groups for purpose of higher studies. Libraries of research institutions, industrial establishments, etc. are classified as special libraries.

TABLE 2.1: **Statewise Distribution of Librarians: According to Census of India, 1971.**

State/Union Territories	Total No. of librarians	% of total population of librarians	Librarians per 1000 persons	Sexwise distribution within State/U.T. Male %	Female %	Distribution in urban area %
Andhra Pradesh	875	7.4	0.02	81.7	18.3	60.0
Assam	165	1.4	0.01	87.9	12.1	57.6
Bihar	519	4.4	0.01	93.3	6.7	79.0
Gujarat	490	4.1	0.02	80.7	19.3	91.8
Haryana	145	1.2	0.01	82.8	17.2	86.2
Himachal Pradesh	170	1.4	0.05	90.6	9.4	28.2
Jammu & Kashmir	84	0.7	0.02	85.7	14.3	90.0
Kerala	720	6.1	0.03	87.5	12.5	36.11
Madhya Pradesh	495	4.2	0.01	91.9	8.1	98.0
Maharashtra	1145	9.6	0.02	74.2	25.8	98.2
Mysore (Karnataka)	580	4.9	0.02	77.6	22.4	89.7
Orissa	450	3.8	0.02	95.5	4.5	40.0
Punjab	230	1.9	0.02	80.4	19.6	82.6
Rajasthan	366	3.1	0.01	91.8	8.2	86.0
Tamil Nadu	1210	10.1	0.03	88.4	11.6	35.1
Uttar Pradesh	1035	8.7	0.01	87.9	12.1	88.4
West Bengal	1574	13.2	0.04	83.8	16.2	69.0
Delhi	1343	11.3	0.33	65.4	34.6	77.3
Other States/ Union Territories	287	2.4	0.04	77.7	22.3	80.8
ALL INDIA	11883			98.21	20.62	87.76
PERCENTAGE		100.0		82.6	17.4	73.8

To represent the three organisational types, viz., *autonomous*, *heteronomous* and *professional departments*, in which librarians work, the *Indian Library Directory* and the *Directory of Special and Research Libraries* were consulted for drawing a list of libraries in Delhi. There are six universities in Delhi, three of them are Central Universities;[7] and the remaining three are in the field of agriculture (Indian Agricultural Research Institute), engineering (Indian Institute of Technology), and health sciences (All India Institute of Medical Sciences). Libraries of these universities may be classified as *autonomous organisation*. From among the Central Universities, the University of Delhi and the Jamia Millia Islamia being the older of the three were included in the sample. The University of Delhi has also the maximum strength of professionals working in its library system.[8]

In the case of public libraries, two libraries viz., Delhi Public Library (DPL) (including its branches) and the Central Secretariat Library (CSL) were selected. Other public libraries were not included because none of them had enough trained librarians to yield meaningful data regarding some aspects like colleaguial relationship, for instance. If one goes strictly by the definition of public library, it may not be appropriate to categorise the CSL under this category. In fact, the CSL administratively is attached to the Ministry of Human Resource Development, Government of India and is primarily meant for the officials and staff of the ministries and the subordinate offices of the Union Government. But there are two factors which prompted us to include it under the category of public library. Firstly, the character of the library has changed and even the common citizens are allowed to make use of it, within its premises. Secondly, the clientele and their background are not in any way different from that of any public library. It may also be worthwhile to mention the criteria under which we consider the Delhi Public Library and the Central Secretariat Library as *heteronomous organisations*. The former is governed by the Delhi Library Board and the latter is attached to the Ministry of Human Resource Development. Yet they are quite similar in respect of internal rules of governance, supervision and service conditions.

In regard to special libraries which we consider as *professional departments*, the investigator identified 15, accounting for 20 per cent of the total, based on multiple criteria. These are, their 'national' importance, nature of their specialised collection, strength of professional staff, number of clientele, budgetary provisions, etc. The details about the libraries included in the sample have been presented in Appendix I. The number of professional staff in these libraries varies between four and twenty-five.

SELECTION OF TRAINED LIBRARIANS

Generally three categories of personnel perform their prescribed roles in the libraries. These are, professionals, para-professionals and non-professionals. The last category, i.e., non-professionals, is common to all organisations which includes, clerks, typists, etc. The other two categories are specifically meant for performing library jobs. These categories differ in terms of their levels of general education and professional education or training. The trained librarians are professionals who hold at least a postgraduate bachelor's degree in library and information science. On the other hand, para-professionals are under-graduates, who generally hold a certificate or diploma in library science, which is a course of shorter duration. As the study is concerned with librarians as professionals only the first category is included in the sample.

On the basis of information available in the Directories[9] the estimated number of trained librarians in Delhi was 753 and the number in the 22 selected libraries was 355 constituting 47.1 per cent of total.

In libraries, work is usually organised on the basis of different sections or divisions. The nomenclature used to identify the sections or divisions may vary but most common sections in a typical library are: Acquisition, Processing, Maintenance, Circulation and/or Reference, Periodicals and/or Documentation and Administration. The working of a section or division is usually supervised by a senior or middle level professional. In a section or division, most of the junior librarians, para-professionals and non-professionals perform their prescribed jobs.

This study includes all the trained librarians who were holding various positions and representing different sections in the 22 libraries.

Professional librarians working in different types of libraries have dissimilar designations and salary structures. They perform their roles at different levels of hierarchies in the libraries. It is easy to recognise three or four levels at which they are placed in a typical library. On the basis of their comparable positions, designations and salary structures, it is possible to group them into three levels or ranks, viz., senior, middle and junior (Appendix II). Like any other organisations, the number of persons at the junior level are larger as compared to middle or senior levels.

ADMINISTRATION OF QUESTIONNAIRES

Our field investigation began with preliminary visits to the libraries, for obtaining latest lists of the professional staff along with relevant background information on the libraries. These lists were scrutinised and professional qualifications of the staff were checked. In this process the estimated figure of 355 trained librarians was reduced to 302 to whom finally the questionnaires were administered.

In all 203 filled in questionnaires were collected back, yielding a response rate of 67.2 per cent. The non-responses were mainly from the senior ranks and women professionals.

All the returned 203 questionnaires were finally checked. Three questionnaires were found unusable because of many non-responses. Ultimately 200 questionnaires were accepted for analysis.

TYPE OF DATA COLLECTED

The nature of data required for a study is determined by its objectives. For present study, what was required, was the following data on:

1. socio-economic background of librarians;
2. occupational careers of librarians which include choice of occupation, career mobility, career satisfaction, self-perception of occupational status;
3. role images, role-perceptions, value orientation in role-perceptions, role-obligations, role-relations in organisation, role-commitment, clients' perception of professionals' role;
4. bureaucratic and professional characteristics of libraries and librarians based on the professionals' perceptions.

The librarians' responses constituted the main source for the data. Barring factual information on background characteristics and some other aspects of occupational career, most other data collected from them were behavioural or perceptual at the cognitive level. As human behaviour originates at the cognitive level, such data are an invaluable source for understanding it.

CONSTRUCTION OF QUESTIONNAIRES

The two types of structured questionnaires were used for the collections of data. The contents of the first questionnaire, which was to be administered to the trained librarians, fell into four broad areas corresponding to the data needs, as indicated above. Another questionnaire, which was meant for collecting data from user-groups, (a sample of 200 users from five university libraries included in the study) contained only selected items the responses to which could indicate the users' perception regarding ideal and actual roles of professional librarians.

Likert scales were used for assessing the nature of bureaucratisation and the degree of professionalisation existed in the organisations or among the sample of librarians. According to the requirement of format, the responses were structured in a graded fashion, such as 'strongly agree', 'agree', 'cannot say', 'disagree' and "strongly disagree'. The number of items to be considered for measuring a particular dimension and type of response categories to be provided for recording the same would necessarily vary according to the problem.

The questionnaire also provided some open-ended questions where responses could not be structured. Before administering the questionnaire to the respondents, it was pre-tested over a sub-sample drawn from one library which was not covered in the study.

SCORING AND TREATMENT OF DATA

According to the objectives of the study, it was desirable to discover the relationship between or among variables and between them and the background characteristics of librarians. The use of Likert scales adopted for assessing the presence or absence of the dimensions in the libraries (organisations) or among the sample of librarians (professionals) were useful for the analysis of association between different variables. Based on the set of items related to a particular dimension, it was intended to construct index or scale for the same dimensions. The method of finding relationship between the variables with the help of such indices can be considered to be somewhat unrefined.

For the purpose of rating the respondents studied on a particular scale, a threefold classification of respondents into 'high', 'moderate' and 'low' was adopted. The threefold classification afforded identification of respondents with distinctly 'high' scores and distinctly 'low' scores with reference to a dimension studied and an examination of the differences between the two. In order to create such groupings, the responses which were recorded on a five point scale were collapsed into three categories, viz. positive ('strongly agree' and 'agree') negative ('disagree' and 'strongly disagree') and neutral ('cannot say'). The respondents who held positive views to the dimension were assigned high score or weight ('strongly agree' and 'agree' – 3); those whose responses were negative to the dimension were given low score ('disagree' and 'strongly disagree' – 1) and the neutrals were assigned middle score ('cannot say' – 2). While considering the cut-off points for 'high', 'moderate' and 'low' categories, the distribution of respondents on the score were kept in view. The cut-off points were decided in such a way that approximately 33 per cent of respondents securing low on the scores should be covered under 'low' group and approximately another 33 per cent of respondents securing high on the scores should fall into the 'high' category and the remaining 34 per cent of respondents should be considered in a 'moderate' category. For example, the scores obtained by respondent on the dimension of 'Content of role commitment' are shown in Table 2.2.

TABLE 2.2: **Score on the Dimension of 'Content of Role Commitment'**

Level	Score	Absolute Frequency	Relative Frequency	Cumulative Frequency
Low	3	26	13.0	13.0
	4	39	19.5	32.5
Moderate	5	27	13.5	46.0
	6	37	18.5	64.5
High	7	28	14.0	78.5
	8	26	13.0	91.5
	9	17	8.5	100.0
Total		200	100.0	

The respondent whose scores varies between seven and nine were placed as 'high'. It is obvious that 35.5 per cent of respondents constitute the 'high' group; similarly 32.5 per cent of respondents who score between 'three and four' were classified in 'low' group and the rest 32.0 per cent of respondents who score between 'five and six' were classified in 'moderate' group. The same methodology for deciding cut-off points, though quite arbitrary in nature, was followed uniformly.

For the purpose of examining the associations between the variables, the following indices were constructed. The items for indices and the percentage of respondents constituting 'high', 'medium' and 'low' groups have been dealt with in relevant chapters.

(1) Content of Role Commitment Index
(2) Index of Centralisation
(3) Index of Specialisation
(4) Index of Formalisation
(5) Index of work-related Autonomy and Utilisation of Professional Knowledge and Skill

(6) Client-Orientation Index.

The information gleaned was coded, computer-processed and analysed to yield the various tables and findings. First of all basic tables were prepared in the form of frequency distribution. On that basis, analysis-plan was drawn out and cross-tabulation of data was undertaken. For considering the association between two variables, percentage analysis was used.

NOTES

1. *The Indian Library Directory* (4th ed.), Delhi: Indian Library Association, 1985.
2. Based on the figures provided in the *Directory of Special and Research Libraries in India*, (Calcutta: IASLIC, 1985).
3. Estimate based on the information available in the *Indian Library Directory* and *The Directory of Special and Research Libraries in India*, op. cit.
4. *Census of India, 1981, Series-1, India, Part II Special* (Reports and Tables Based on 5 per cent Sample Data), Delhi: Registrar General and Census Commissioner for India, 1983.
5. *Census of India, 1981, Series 28, Delhi, Part III – A and B and Part IV-A*, Delhi: Director of Census Operations 1985.
6. The State-wise classification of occupations for 1981 Census in not available as yet, so the information is based on 1971 Census. See, *Census of India, Series-1, India, Part II-B(VI), Vol. I and II, Economic Tables (Tables B.V.)*, Delhi: Registrar General and Census Commissioner for India, 1977.
7. The University of Delhi was established in the year 1922. The Jamia Millia Islamia established in 1920 was deemed to be university up to Feb. 1989. Afterwards, it became the Central University. The Jawaharlal Nehru University, though established in 1968, started functioning from 1971.
8. The number of professional staff in Delhi University Library System is 93.
9. *The Indian Library Directory and the Directory of Special and Research Libraries* were used for finding out the information regarding professional librarians of Delhi. The figure 753 was arrived at by counting the number of professional staff mentioned under the name of each library located in the city of Delhi. Further a separate count was made for ascertaining the number of professional librarians working in those libraries which were included in the sample, as noted in Appendix I.

THREE

LIBRARIANSHIP IN INDIA: A HISTORICAL PERSPECTIVE

THE OCCUPATIONAL role of librarians in ancient and medieval times was chiefly concerned with the collection of documents as cultural heritage. During most of its history, librarianship has lacked some of the major characteristics of a profession.[1] The growth of modern librarianship in the West can be traced from the last quarter of the nineteenth century. The process of professionalisation of librarianship started with the foundation of the American Library Association in the U.S.A. in 1876 and the Library Association in U.K. in 1877.[2] The first Library School was established in 1877 by Melvil Dewey at the LIbrary of Columbia College in the U.S.A. In U.K., the first formal training for librarians was started by the Library Association. The Library Association (in U.K.) also set up an official register of librarians in 1909.[3] In 1933 Pierce Butler wrote *Introduction to Library Science*.[4] Thereafter many significant developments took place in the profession which established its claim for the profession. Today librarianship is characterised by systematic professional education; proliferation of professional literature; adoption and innovation of different tools and techniques for sophisticated handling of information needs of various categories of users and management of different types of libraries/information centres.

In India, the profession of librarianship began to emerge during past fifty years.[5] Needless to mention that India had a rich tradition of libraries in the past. References to libraries are very common in the ancient and medieval literature. Libraries attached to the ancient universities such as Takshsila, Nalanda, Vikramsila etc. were sources to classical education. During medieval period the Moghul emperors, nobles and courtiers had their personal libraries. With the rise of European settlements in the seventeenth and eighteenth centuries, libraries became a part of social and educational institutions. By the end of nineteenth century, the three provincial capitals of India — Bombay,

Calcutta and Madras –and many of the towns had their public libraries.

In the beginning of the twentieth century, the concept of public library was first recognised by the British Government. In 1901, the Government declared open the Imperial Library (now the National Library) to the public.[6] From 1900 onwards, India witnessed a strong movement for the establishment of libraries in different parts of the country. The officials of the provincial governments, the rulers of the princely states, eminent citizens and the librarians played an active role in the library movement. The first significant contribution was made by Maharaja Sayajirao III, the then ruler of the State of Baroda. In 1910, he introduced a scheme for public library service in his State. With the establishment of Indian Library Association in 1933, the cause of library movement was rapidly advanced. A model Library Act drafted by Dr. Ranganathan was introduced in the Bengal Legislature (1931). Similar Library Bills were introduced in Madras, Bombay and Travancore. In 1939, the Government of Bombay appointed a Library Committee for the development of public libraries in the whole State.

In the post-independence era, libraries became instruments for accelerating the process of social change, education and development. The national government took first step in that direction by declaring the (Imperial Library of Calcutta) as the National Library of India in 1948. The public library movement was given a fillip through the Scheme of Improvement of Library Service in the Five Year Plan of Educational Development. Later on library developments formed part of the national plans of India. Thereafter, library associations (of both State and national levels) and individual librarians made collective efforts for the enactment of library legislation. Consequently the first Library Act (1948) was passed by the State of Madras in 1950. In 1954, Government of India enacted the Delivery of Books (Public Library Act, 1954). In 1955, international cooperation was sought for the library development. With the efforts of UNESCO, a model public library was established in Delhi (known as Delhi Public Library). In 1957, the Government of India constituted an Advisory Committee for Libraries which submitted its report about the future set-up of library development and library education in the country. The committee also advocated the need for library legislation for all the States of India. But in spite of the consistent efforts made by library associations, only five States in India – viz., Tamil Nadu (1948), Andhra Pradesh (1966), Karnataka (1966), Maharashtra (1967) and West Bengal (1981) – have achieved success in enacting library legislation. In 1972, the Central

Government has taken a major step by establishing Raja Rammohun Roy Library Foundation – an autonomous body – for supporting the library development in the country.[7] The library profession is now earnestly making an effort for the planned growth of library and information science in India. On its initiative the Government of India recently constituted a Committee for National Policy on Library and Information Science which submitted its interim report in 1986.[8] The *Report of the Working Group of the Planning Commission on Modernisation of Library Services and Information for the Seventh Five Year Plan 1985-90* is a big achievement for the library profession in India.[9]

ACADEMIC LIBRARIANSHIP

Before Independence, there were only 17 universities in India.[10] The objectives of the establishment of universities were not so much for the advancement of learning and research as for conducting examinations and awarding degrees. As a result many of the universities and colleges had poor library facilities. After Independence Government of India appointed University Education Commission (1948) under the Chairmanship of Dr. Radhakrishnan. The Commission took cognizance of the deplorable conditions of academic libraries and specified their role in the following words:

> The Library is the heart of all the University's work; directly so as regards its research work, and indirectly as regards its educational work. Scientific research needs a library as well as its laboratories while for humanistic research, the library is both the library and laboratory in one.[11]

The University Grants Commission (UGC) which was set up in 1953 as a result of the recommendation of the University Education Commission devoted proper attention towards the development of academic libraries from its inception. The UGC appointed a library committee (1957) under the Chairmanship of Dr. S.R. Ranganathan. The recommendations of the Library Committee (1959) formed the basis of development of academic librarianship in India. The Committee prepared a comprehensive report covering almost all aspects of university libraries.[12] With its the scene of the academic libraries has changed drastically. But developments in academic libraries were not uniform. Many of the academic libraries lacked proper financial support from their State governments. Imbalances were evident in collection, development, staff-strength and pattern of services. More recently rising cost of reading materials have resulted in inadequate funds causing many academic librarians to search for new ways and means to meet the challenges. The Association of Indian Universities took initiative in 1986 to formulate a National Policy on University Libraries.[13] More concretely in 1989, the Inter Agency Working Group of the University Grants Commission suggested for setting up an Information and Library Network (*INFLIBNET*) which can inter-connect the people and resources of all universities, institutes of higher education and research laboratories.

ROLE AND STATUS OF ACADEMIC LIBRARIANS

Academic Librarians were accorded inferior status during late nineteenth and early twentieth centuries because of custodial, clerical or housekeeping roles they performed. It was further supported by low educational background of librarians and smaller size of the libraries. After World War II, the rapid growth in academic libraries brought the need for specialisation and expert assistance in locating information. The pattern of library and information science education also provided new entrants to the profession a variety of bibliographical tools, reference and research materials. Libraries were forced to create new conditions and innovate new methods for enhancing the utilisation of existing resources for their clients. Many new concepts, such as user education, 'bibliographic instruction', 'College-library', 'independent study', etc. were developed for the purpose of motivating the clients for the use of libraries.[14] Librarians were thus led to believe that their roles were equal to teachers though they did not hold any formal classes.[15] Improved qualifications of librarians facilitated the way for achieving of their faculty status. The demand for status was so widely discussed and debated that it resulted into the proliferation of a great deal of literature on the subject.[16] The three important American associations, i.e., (i) The Association of College and Research Libraries; (ii) The Association of American Colleges and (iii) The American Association of University Professors accepted the following roles of librarians:

> Librarians perform a teaching and research role inasmuch as they instruct student formally and informally and advise and assist

> faculty in their scholarly pursuits. Librarians are also themselves involved in the research function; many conduct research in their own professional interests and in the discharge of their duties.[17]

As a result of the acceptance of the above roles, today in the U.S.A. almost 79 per cent of academic librarians have some sort of faculty status.[18] Like U.S.A., in Canada university librarians were also granted academic status in the university on the grounds that they are professional members of the university staff with advanced academic training, the criteria accepted in matters of promotion, appointment and tenure; . . .[19]

In U.K., the University Grants Committee (1963-64) also recommended that "the graduate members of the senior staff should be give equal status and emoluments with the academic staff".[20]

Back home, academic librarians in India are greatly indebted to Dr. S.R. Ranganathan for their, enhanced academic status and salary scales. As head of the Library Committee of the University Grants Commission, Dr. Ranganathan defined the status and salary of library staff unambiguously:

> The high academic and professional qualification, the combination of academic and administrative responsibilities and the practice in the university all the world over indicate that the status and the salary scale of library staff should be the same as that of the teaching and research staff.[21]

The recommendation of the Library Committee was accepted by the University Grants Commission in its entirety. The UGC annual report clearly stated that the report of the Ranganathan Committee and the report of the Seminar on *Workflow in Libraries* (1959) has been adopted and were "to form the basis for guidance in the construction, development and administration of university libraries".[22] As a result, the professional library staff was placed at par with academic staff in universities and colleges at the time of revision of pay scales during 1961 and 1966. But, however, in 1973, the University Grants Commission took a very unfavourable attitude towards librarians. The Commission decided to delink the principle of parity in respect of salary and status of professional library staff.[23] The academic libraries all over the country were aggrieved by this decision. They immediately initiated a wide debate for restoration of their status and their resentment was expressed through various memoranda, symposia, seminars and conferences. A National Convention of University and College Librarians was held in Delhi (1975).[24] In order to continue the struggle for parity of status, members of the convention formed a new forum called Indian Association of Academic Librarians (INDAAL) in 1977. In addition, some individual librarians also resorted to legal action.[25]

While librarians were fighting their battle with the UGC, authorities of some Central and State universities took a favourable attitude in respect of providing academic grades to their professional librarians. Some of the State universities, with the approval of their State governments, even ignoring the direction of UGC, gave recognition to their qualified library professional staff as teachers.[26] Ultimately, the UGC and the Central Government had to reconsider their decisions. They agreed in principle to upgrade the status of the librarians from April 1980.[27] At present all the academic librarians working in the Central universities and majority of them working in State universities are accorded/or in the process of being accorded parity with teachers. In 1984 the University Grants Commission also extended the Merit Promotion Scheme to librarians, as it was made applicable to the teachers. The UGC informed all universities that "where a University, in accordance with Acts and Statutes, has declared the Librarians/Documentation Officers as teachers, without affecting the fact that they are non-vacation academic staff, such teachers may be considered for purposes of Merit Promotion in accordance with the UGC guidelines. . . ."[28]

SPECIAL LIBRARIANSHIP

The phenomenal growth of special libraries can be witnessed only in the twentieth century, though its history may be traced back to the 19th century.[29] In the United States the special libraries began to appear around 1820. In U.K. also, the demand for industrial and social progress created a special interest in the establishment of special libraries during 19th century. India had very few special libraries during that time. The learned societies and associations were slow to grow because the priorities of research were to be decided by the foreigners. It was only during the first half of the twentieth century that research organisations began to be established. These organisations in turn created their own libraries and information centres for the promotion of research and development. But it was only after independence that programmes for planned scientific, industrial and socio-economic developments were formulated and libraries information centres were considered necessary infrastructure for research development.[30] Today, developments in special librarianship have taken place to such an extent that each sector of research or development is supported by a network of information system.[31] Attempts are also being made to establish linkages with international information system for sharing of information on worldwide basis.[32]

PROFESSIONAL EDUCATION

The first training programme for librarians in India was organised in 1910 by W.A. Borden who came here to plan the library development for the erstwhile state of Baroda on the initiative of Maharaja Sayajirao III.[33] In 1915, the Punjab University, Lahore (now in Pakistan) introduced a systematic curriculum for the training of librarians. But the actual foundation of library science education was laid down by Dr. S.R. Ranganathan in 1929. A certificate course of three months, duration was started by the Madras Library Association in close cooperation of the University of Madras. On the pattern of Madras University, many other universities also started the certificate courses. The first one year post-graduate diploma course in library science was introduced by Dr. Ranganathan in the University of Madras in 1929. The other universities which followed the model of University of Madras for the one year diploma course were Banaras Hindu University (1941), University of Bombay (1944), Calcutta University (1946), and University of Delhi (1947). At the time of independence there were thus only five universities which were conducting diploma courses in the library science.[34]

After Independence, the need for trained professional librarians was felt urgently as new libraries and information centres were coming up. The programme of National Development and Reconstruction started in 1951 along with the Five Year Plan provided the stimulus for the growth of libraries. The first full-time professor in library science was also appointed by the University of Delhi with the initiative of Sir Maurice Gwyer, the then Vice-Chancellor of the University. At present more than 75 per cent of the universities have full-time faculty and more than 60 universities are conducting library science courses at graduate level.[35] There are twenty universities which have a further one year course leading to Master Degree in Library Science. More than nine universities offer Ph.D. programme in Library and Information Science.

The standard of library science education is being constantly reviewed by various professional organisations and the UGC. The latter made a comprehensive report on library science education in 1965.[36] In addition to that, it has a panel on Library and Information Science to review the different aspects of education in respect of status of library schools, financial supports, physical facilities, curriculum etc.[37]

PROFESSIONAL ORGANISATIONS

In India, the library associations came into being along with the development of libraries during the second decade of this century. The State associations were first to appear before any national associations could come up.[38] The first library association was established in Andhra Pradesh in 1914. The Andhra Pradesh Library Association convened the First All India Public Library Conference at Madras in 1919 which encouraged the growth of other State library associations. Before the emergence of Indian Library Association in 1933, the State associations, which actively promoted the cause of Library Movement in the country, were Maharashtra Library Association (1921), Bengal Library Association (1925), Madras Library Association (1928), Punjab Library Association (1929), Uttar Pradesh Library Association (1935), Assam Library Association (1939), Bihar Library Association (1940), Utkal Library Association (1944) and Kerala Granthalaya Sangam (1945).[39]

It was mentioned above that the first attempt of forming a national body of librarians was made as early as 1919. As a result, All India Public Library Association (AIPLA) was formed. Though AIPLA worked for some time, its activities did not satisfy a group of librarians and intellectuals who were in search of some strong professional association. Dr. M.O. Thomas pleaded in *Modern Librarian* that "for an Indian Library Movement a strong vanguard of All India Library Association is absolutely needed."[40] In this process the ILA was born at the time of All India Library Conference in Calcutta in September 1933. The main objective of the Association was to create an apex body of librarians and literary workers to propagate the development of libraries at national level. From its inception, the ILA was engaged in professional activities. During the Presidentship of Dr. S.R.

Ranganathan (1944-53), the Association had performed many new activities. After independence, the ILA has been actively representing the profession at the national level. It is engaged in improving the functioning of libraries; status, salary and working conditions of the library professionals. The Association paid its befitting tribute to Dr. Ranganathan by organising an International Conference on the Philosophy of Ranganathan in 1982 (in Delhi).[41]

Like any other professional body, the ILA was concerned with the holding of regular conferences, seminars, symposia and workshops. The Association started the publication of its first professional journal entitled *Library Bulletin* in 1942. In 1949 another learned periodical *Abgila* was started. In 1964, the *ILA Bulletin* was started. From 1984, the Association also felt the need for publishing its *newsletter*.

Another national level association formed before independence (1933) is Government of India Librarians Association (GILA) which is now Association of Government Librarians and Information Specialists (AGLIS). The Association looks after the interests of librarians working in the ministries and various departments of the Government of India. It has been very active in matters of raising salary and status of the librarians working in various government organisations.

After independence, Indian Association of Special Libraries and Information Centre (IASLIC) (1955) was formed. The objective was to deal with the problems of scientific, technical and research libraries and documentation centres. The professional activities of IASLIC are more specialised as compared to the ILA. It also holds regular conferences and conducts courses on modern themes of library and information science.

In addition to the ILA, AGLIS, IASLIC and INDAAL, there are other associations which represent a special group of librarians and information scientists such as Medical Library Association of India (MLAI), Association of Agricultural Librarians and Documentalists of India (AALDI), etc. The teachers of library science also have an association known as the Indian Association of Teachers of Library Science (IATLIS) which was formed in 1969. These associations serve the special interests of their members.

Today librarians are better organised through their national and State level associations. They strive for higher standard of professional education and training; better status and salary; library legislation, a code of ethics, work norms, and above all for a National Policy of

Library and Information Science.

Thus, Indian librarianship has made sufficient progress within its short history. As new technology is going to change the traditional pattern of libraries, it is heartening to note that Indian librarianship is also not lagging behind and from the middle of 1980s important research and academic libraries are moving towards computerisation.[42]

Library profession in India has also made some unique contributions to world librarianship.[43] These contributions were made by Dr. S.R. Ranganathan who is regarded as Einstein in the field of library science. Prior to Ranganathan, library science was devoid of a basic philosophy. The rule of thumb was the order of the day. But the publication of *Five Laws of Library Science* provided the ethical, philosophical and service base of the profession.[44] Professional education has also been enriched with the addition of new course on 'universe of knowledge' originally designed by Ranganathan.[45] For a new theory of classification and indexing, the world librarianship is greatly indebted to India.[46]

PROFESSIONALISATION OF LIBRARIANSHIP

The evolution of librarianship, as presented above in brief, indicates that librarianship has moved towards professionalisation. This may be said emphatically for both Indian and world librarianship. But it is a matter of great concern for librarians that their profession does not measure well in terms of professional characteristics. In this regard first of all Goode had examined the occupation of librarians and found that it lacked (a) prolonged specialised training in a body of abstract knowledge and (b) a collectivity or service orientation.[47] About the same time, Shaffer analysed librarianship in terms of 19 attributes and concluded that it was still in the infantile stage of professional development.[48] Bundy and Wasserman had found that librarianship was making slow progress in acquiring professional status.[49] Both Gwinup[50] and North[51] noticed the failure of librarians to reach professional status because of the weakness of four components of professionalism: the service ideal, a body of esoteric knowledge, professional association and public image. According to Asheim, librarianship was lacking a great deal in respect of community sanction.[52] Merchant was also convinced that professional roles of librarians were short on intellectual challenge, reward and growth because of sterile role training.[53] Interestingly librarians' passion for professionalism generated an enormous amount of literature in the library science field.[54] The debate over professionalism provided them an opportunity for soul searching. In the process of introspection, librarians have been able to identify their areas of failures. Two important aspects in this case are: professional role and professional education. It has been widely observed in libraries that professional roles are inadequately structured. Usually librarians perform more routine and regulative activities in organisations which are lacking in autonomy, individual judgement, and expertise. Such roles are more bureaucratic rather than professional in content.[55] Most of these remain undefined and ambiguous. As such their relations with the clients become indirect or fragmentary. Clients are thus found to be ignored or discouraged from interaction. They are often considered as problems, as source of disorder, rather than as source of direction.[56]

For a profession, a systematic body of knowledge is considered an indispensable attribute. A profession cannot advance further if its knowledge base is narrow. In librarianship, it has been realised that its knowledge base is neither large nor complex enough to permit the profession to make adequate service to the clients.[57] Even today, professional education in librarianship concentrates on only traditional core curriculum, though with changed nomenclature.[58] Library science students are taught more 'techniques' rather than 'theory'. Even library science educators fail to make distinction between 'theory' and 'technique'. Moreover whatever theory they teach, they fail to integrate it into practice.[59]

Another area which is more disturbing to the librarians concerns their low public image.[60] For the public, libraries are indispensable but not the librarians. The public often fails to distinguish between professional librarians and others working in libraries because of lack of demarcation between professional and non-professional activities. There are also many unfavourable images or stereotypes associated with the occupation of librarians.[61] Librarians are viewed as 'conservative', 'ritualistic', 'passive', 'unimaginative', etc.[62] In society they are regarded as 'clerks' and 'second class citizens' and in organisations, they lack power and autonomy.[63]

While admitting the limitations of the profession, librarians are now convinced that by using the criteria of traditional professions, librarianship will never be accorded the status of a profession.[64] For example, librarianship will not be in a position to prescribe to clients and clients will also not be willing to accept the authority of the professional. Thus, the criterion of pıofessional authority, as applied to other professions, may not be valid for librarianship.[65] On the contrary, librarianship is endowed with some unique characteristics such as 'organisation of knowledge', 'access to information' etc., which need to be well preserved and enlarged in context of the changing needs of the society. The same would provide the profession its due recognition, as we know that the hallmark of post-industrial society is knowledge and information.[66]

NOTES

1. Howard W. Winger (1964), "Aspects in Librarianship: A Trace Work of History", in Philip H. Ennis and Howard W. Winger (eds.), *Seven Questions About the Profession of Librarianship*, Chicago: The University of Chicago, p. 23.
2. Dale Engene Shaffar (1968), *The Maturity of Librarianship as a Profession*, Metuchen, N.J.: The Scareerew Press, p. 68.
3. James Thompson (1977), *A History of the Principles of Librarianship*, London: Clive Bingley, p. 116.
4. Pierce Butler (1971), *Introduction to Library Science*, Chicago: University of Chicago Press.
5. See P. B. Mangla (1983) et al., (eds.), *Fifty Years of Librarianship in India, Past, Present and Future* (Seminar Papers Twentieth Ninth All India Library Conference, Mysore University, December 5-9, 1983), Delhi: Indian Library Association.
6. See Jogesh Mishra (1979), *History of Libraries and Librarianship Since 1850*, Delhi: Atma Ram, pp. 52-104.
7. See *Raja Rammohun Roy Library Foundation Newsletter*, Vol. 6, (1 and 2), 1986.
8. *ILA Newsletter*, Vol. 3(2), 1986, p. 7.
9. Girja Kumar (1985), *Towards a National Information Policy* (Thirtieth All India Library Conference, Jaipur, January 28-31, 1985, Presidential Address), Delhi: Indian Library Association, pp. iv-v.
10. K.A. Isaac (1983), "Development of University Library in India", in P. B. Mangla et al., (eds.), op. cit., pp. 40-52.
11. India, University Education Commission, December 1948 — August 1949, *Report*, pp. 110-13.
12. University Grants Commission (India), *University and College Libraries Containing the Report of the Library Committee of the U.G.C. and the Proceedings of the Seminar on From Publisher to Reader held on March 4-7, 1959*, New Delhi: UGC, 1965.
13. Association of Indian Universities, *Proceedings, 61st Annual Meeting*, November 8-11, 1986, New Delhi, AIU, 1986.
14. See Girja Kumar and Krishan Kumar (1983), *Philosophy of User Education*, Delhi: Vikas.
15. Pauline Wilson (1979), "Librarians as Teachers: The Study of an Organisation Fiction", *Library Quarterly*, Vol. 49, pp. 146-52.

16. See N. Datta (1985), *Academic Status for University and College Librarians in India*, Delhi: Indian Bibliographies, p. 6 and pp. 189-204.
17. See Jagdish Saran Sharma (1986), *Library Movement in India and Abroad*, New Delhi: Ess Ess Publications, pp. 198-99.
18. John N. DePew (1983), The ACRL Standards for Faculty Status: Panacea or Placebo, *College and Research Libraries*, Vol. 44, pp. 407-20.
19. Jagdish Saran Sharma (1986), op. cit., p. 199.
20. *Ibid.*, p. 198.
21. See University Grants Commission (India), op. cit., pp. 63-69.
22. *Ibid., Report for the Year 1959-60*, pp. 14-15.
23. See N. Datta (1985), op. cit., p. 54.
24. National Convention of University and College Librarians (New Delhi) (1975), *Faculty Status for University and College Librarians in India: Basic Documents*, New Delhi, 1975.
25. See N. Datta (1985), op. cit., p. 58.
26. J.K. Anand (1985), "Academic Status of University and College Librarians in India: A Retrospective Study", P. B. Mangla et al., (eds.), op. cit., pp. 83-103.
27. *Ibid.*
28. *ILA Newsletter*, Vol. 1(1), April-May, 1984, pp. 3-4.
29. A.K. Mukherjee (1969), *Fundamental of Special Librarianship and Documentation*, Calcutta, IASLIC.
30. Jogesh Mishra (1974), op. cit., pp. 56-57.
31. P. B. Mangla (1983), "Forward", in P. B. Mangla et al., (eds.), op. cit., p. viii.
32. B.M. Gupta (1986), et al., (eds.), *Handbook of Libraries, Archives and Information Centres in India*, Vol. 3, New Delhi: Information Industry Publication, p. 255.
33. Jagdish Saran Sharma (1986), op. cit., p. 177.
34. P. B. Mangla (1984-85), "Library and Information Science Education in India" in B.M. Gupta et al., (eds.), *Handbook of Libraries, Archives and Information Centres in India*, Vol. 1, New Delhi: Information Industry Publications, pp. 239.
35. *Ibid.*, p. 248.
36. University Grants Commission (India), *Library Science in Indian Universities: Report of the University Grants Commission Review Committee*, New Delhi: UGC, 1965, p. 86.
37. See Jagdish Saran Sharma (1986), op. cit., p. 179.
38. B.L. Bhardwaj (1986), "Library Associations of India" in B.M. Gupta et al., (eds.), *Handbook of Libraries, Archives and Information Centres in India*, Vol. 2, New Delhi: Information Industry Publication, pp. 755-66.
39. P. N. Kaula (1958), *Library Movement in India*: Delhi, Delhi Library Association.
40. See *50 Years of Indian Library Association, 1933-1983* (Golden Jubilee), Delhi: Indian Library Association, 1983, p. 15.
41. T.S. Rajagopalan (1986) (ed.), *Ranaganthan's Philosophy: Assessment, Impact and Relevance*, Delhi, Vikas, p. 690.
42. See P.S.G. Kumar (1987), *Computerisation of Indian Libraries*, Delhi: B.R. Publishing, p. 334.
43. P. N. Kaula (1986), "Contributions of Ranganathan and World Librarianship", in T.S. Rajagopalan (ed.), *Ranganathan's Philosophy . . .*, op. cit., pp. 28-40.
44. Anis Khurshid (1986), "Ranganathan's Search for a Normative Base in Librarian-

ship" in T.S. Rajagopalan (ed.), *Ranganathan's Philosophy* . . ., op. cit., pp. 41-50.

45. P. N. Kaula (1986), "Contributions of Ranganathan and World Librarianship", op. cit., p. 32.
46. *Ibid.*, pp. 29-31.
47. William J. Goode (1964), "The Librarian: From Occupation to Professions?" in Philip H. Ennis, and Howard W. Winger, op. cit., pp. 8-22.
48. Dale Eugene Shaffer (1968), op. cit., p. 132.
49. Mary Lee Bundy and Paul Wassermann (1968), "Professionalism Reconsidered", *College and Research Libraries*, Vol. 29(8), pp. 5-26.
50. Thomas Gwinup (1974), "The Failure of Librarians to Attain Profession: The Causes, the Consequences and the Prospect", *Wilson Library Quarterly*, Vol. 48, 1974, pp. 482-91.
51. John North (1977), "Librarianship: A Profession", *Canadian Library Journal*, Vol. 34, pp. 253-57.
52. Lester Asheim (1979), "Librarians as Professional", *Library Trends*, Vol. 27(3), pp. 225-57.
53. Maurice P. Merchant (1984), "A Symposium: The Library professional: An Improved Model", *Journal of Academic Librarianship*, Vol. 10(4), pp. 191-94.
54. See, for example, "Professionalism — An LJ Mini-Symposium", *Library Journal*, Vol. 102, September 1, 1977, pp. 1715-31.
55. David G.E.S. Parks (1980), "Academic Librarianship: Professional Strivings and Political Realities", *College and Research Libraries*, Vol. 41, pp. 408-21.
56. Charles R. Martell (1984), "Myths, Schooling and the Practice Librarianship", *College and Research Libraries*, Vol. 45(5), pp. 374-82.
57. Pauline Wilson (1978), "Impending Change in Library Education: Implications for Planning", *Journal of Education for Librarianship*, Vol. 18, pp. 159-74.
58. Kevin McGarry (1983), "Education for Librarianship and Information Science: A Retrospect and A Revaluation", *Journal of Documentation*, Vol. 39(2), pp. 95-122.
59. Richard L. Derr (1983), "The Integration of Theory and Practice in Professional Programmes", *Journal of Education for Librarianship*, Vol. 23 (2), pp. 193-206.
60. See, G.W. Williams and A.J. Woods (1964), "The Image of the Librarians", *New Library World*, Vol. 75, pp. 168-70; L. Chapman (1980), 'Popular Images", *New Library World*, Vol. 81, pp. 153-54.
61. Peter Dollard (1977), "Look the Loonies in a Stereotype!", *Library Journal*, Vol. 102, September 1, pp. 1724-25.
62. Thomas Gwinup (1974), op. cit., pp 482-91.
63. Narda L. Schwartz (1977), "The professional Attitude", *Library Journal*, Vol. 102, September 1, pp. 1729-173; Peter Dollard (1977), op. cit., pp. 1724-25.
64. William F. Birdsall (1980), "Librarians and Professionalism: Status Measured by Outmoded Models", *Canadian Library Journal*, Vol. 37, pp. 145-48.
65. Gardner Hanks and C. James Schmidt (1975), "An Alternative Model of a Profession for Librarian", *College and Research Libraries*, Vol. 36, pp. 175-87.
66. Pauline Wilson (1978), "Librarianship and ALA in a Post-Industrial Society" *American Libraries*, Vol. 9, pp. 124-28.

FOUR

SOCIO-ECONOMIC BACKGROUND OF LIBRARIANS

THE CLOSE relationship between the social structure and occupations has been emphasised in Chapter One. In order to understand the place of library professionals in social structure, it is necessary to know their social and economic backgrounds from where they are recruited. The role of socio-demographic factors in the formation of human personality and in moulding of attitudes and behaviour cannot be denied. An analysis of such factors would include not only the personal attributes of respondents, their religions, caste, linguistic-regional and rural-urban backgrounds but also their family backgrounds. Such investigation of social environment would help us to understand the relationship between a particular social milieu and the recruitment base of a profession. Further, it would also help us to know how different social categories have availed of the opportunities available to them or how far social structure is modernised for providing the base for recruitment of various social categories into modern professions. Additionally, an enquiry into the family background of respondents—their father's education and occupation, etc., would reveal the social mobility—both intergenerational educational mobility and intergenerational occupational mobility—which these categories are experiencing. Apart from these, some additional information on educational and professional attainments were also required for analysing the impact of these factors on career patterns and professional behaviour of librarians. It is assumed that an investigation of the above factors would be helpful in explaining their role perceptions, role commitments, role-relations and their orientations towards organisations and professions.

SEX DIFFERENTIALS

A study of sex-differentials of an occupation reveals as to what extent the female population participates in that occupation. Librarianship, which is relatively a new profession, has acquired a feminine image in the Western world.[1] The sex typing of an occupation indicates that one sex dominates the occupation in number. It would mean that the percentage of women in an occupation deviates substantially from their percentage in the adult population or in the labour force. Sex typing in the professions seems to be specially prominent in the United States.[2] The ratio of women to men in the elementary school teaching is 5 to 7, but in the higher status profession of college and university teaching, it is reversed in favour of men, 2 to 1; women librarians outnumber men by 5:1 and male physicians outnumber women by 10 to 1. The interesting aspect is that the women have always been under-represented in the higher status occupations. Studies on sex typing in the profession highlight two characteristics: (a) the concentration of females in an occupation tends to lower the prestige of the occupation, and (b) women's occupations have lower wage and salary.[3] It has been noticed from such studies that women are heavily concentrated in non-profit sectors of the economy such as school teaching, nursing, social work and librarianship. The occupations in which women have majority have been characterised by sociologists as semi-professions. It has been suggested that women seem to affect the structure of the profession and tend to impose the "weakness of their sex upon their profession".[4] The feminisation of occupation not only implies that the ratio of women to men is large but that occupation is itself defined in terms of feminine traits.[5]

The feminisation of occupation occurs when women monopolise an occupation, then fewer men apply to such occupations because of low salary and less prestige and consequently that occupation tends to become women's occupation. Some studies on occupational choice have also demonstrated that sex typing and career are closely related. Robinson *et al.*, revealed that people oriented professions contain a large percentage of women than data-oriented professions, though there are exceptions and variations from society to society.[6] In the light of the above generalisations stemming from the studies of developed countries, it would be an interesting task to examine how far Indian Librarianship would measure in terms of women's participation.

Out of 200 librarians covered in the sample, there were 135 (67.5 per cent) men and 65 (32.5 per cent) women. According to Government of India Census, 1981,[7] the women librarians in India constituted 21.7 per cent of the total number of librarians. Delhi has the highest population of women librarians in India, their percentage figures during 1971[8] and 1981,[9] were 34.6 per cent and 41.6 per cent respectively.

Our sample percentage of women librarians seems to be in close confirmity with 1971 Census figure. Apparently the increasing trend of female employment in librarianship, as revealed by 1981 Census data, is not reflected in the sample. It could be that the occupational label "librarian" is not exclusively applied to professional librarian only. The para-professionals who hold certificate in Library and Information Science are usually designated as librarians in many small research libraries, public libraries and school libraries. Therefore, one guess would be that the increased numbers were absorbed in para-professional positions. It was also noted that we had significant non-responses from women librarians.

Further, when we compare the trend of women's employment in the library professions with that of the population of women librarians in our sample, we find that the latter (Table 4.1) reveals almost an identical trend.

TABLE 4.1: **A Comparison of the Population of Female Librarians in Delhi According to Government of India Census with that of the Population of Female Librarians in the Sample of the Study**

Percentage of female librarians in Delhi according to Census		Percentage of female librarians according to their years of entry into the librarianship as covered in the sample	
Census	Percentage	Year of Joining	Percentage
.1961	15.4	Up to 1960	12.5
*1971	34.6	1961-70	29.6
+1981	41.6	1981 onwards	37.6

Sources: .(1) Census of India, 1961, Vol.19, Delhi, Part 2A, B, Part III, Delhi, Supdt. of Census Operations, 1965.

*(2) Census of India, 1971, Series 27, Delhi, Part II-B, General Economic Tables, Delhi, Director of Census Operations, 1981.

+(3) Census of India, 1981, Series 28, Delhi, Part III-A and B and Part IV-A, Delhi: Director of Census Operations, 1985.

Thus, it seems that the sample is representative in respect of women's share in librarianship. This is further confirmed from the data presented by The Degree Holders and Technical Personnel Survey, 1981 which indicates that there are 67.29 male and 32.71 female degree holders personnel in Library Science in India.[10]

In India, generally the representation of women in organised sectors of employment is relatively low. In recent decades, the number of female workers has been growing steadily but slowly. The employment trend among women shows very selective trend as observed by the Committee of the Status of Women.[11] For example, women are largely concentrated in teaching profession, specially in secondary schools (Table 4.2). The second most favourate occupation for women seems to be the librarianship. The data presented in Table 4.2 regarding the employment of women in selected professions including librarianship, clearly indicate that only in the case of library profession that the population of females has increased three times within two decades only. If the same trend is allowed to continue, which is not unlikely, it seems that the feminisation of library profession may occur.

TABLE 4.2: **Participation of Females in some Selected Professions in India*(%)**

Classification of occupations according to Census of India	1961	1971	1981
Architects, Engineers, Technologists and Surveyors	0.4	0.8	1.05
Physicians and Surgeons	5.5	6.8	8.7
Teachers, University and Colleges	14.2	23.5	19.3
Administrative, Executives and Managerial Workers	2.7	1.4	2.5
Teachers, Secondary Schools	22.7	23.5	28.5
Librarians	7.8	17.4	21.7

*Data compiled from the following sources:

(1) Census of India, 1961, Vol. I, India, Part II-B(ii), General Economic Tables, Delhi: Registrar General and Census Commissioner; (2) Census of India, 1971, Series I, India, Part II-B(vi), Vols. I and II, Economic Tables (B-v); Delhi: (3) Census of India, 1981, Series I, India, Part II, Special Reports and Tables on 5 per cent sample data.

AGE STRUCTURE

The age, as it is used in biological sense, is not much of direct relevance to sociologists. But in the chronological sense, it has important sociological implications. It is well known to us that generational difference creates problem in colleaguial and superior-subordinate relations. Further, the age groupings of librarians can also be related to the development of profession and to the amount of experience which the members have had in the profession.

The age-structure of respondents has been presented in Table 4.3. The majority of respondents are in the middle (35 to 44 years) and higher age (45 and above) groups and merely 30 per cent of them are in the young age (25 to 34 years). It is noteworthy that there is preponderence of male librarians in the middle and higher age-groups, while the females are clustered in the young and middle age-groups. That women belong to younger age in large proportion (nearly fifty per cent of them as revealed by the data) can be partly explained by the fact their entry to the profession is relatively new. It also indicates that they have not yet been stabilised in the profession *vis-a-vis* their male counterparts. Another reason for their higher percentage in the young age group may also be attributed to the possibility of their turn-over in the employment. Women often give up their career on marriage and after achieving motherhood to look after their children. So the inflow of younger women may be predicted as a continual process.

F 4.3: **Distribution of Respondents by their Age, Sex and Marital Status (in percentage)**

Age group	Sex (N=200)						
	Male (N=135)			Female (N=65)			Total
	Married	Unmarried	Sub-total	Married	Unmarr-ied	Sub-total	
25-34 (Young)	10.5	4.0	14.5	10.0	5.0	15.0	29.5
35-44 (Middle)	21.0	1.0	22.0	9.5	3.0	12.5	34.5
45 and above (Higher)	30.5	0.5	31.0	4.0	1.0	5.0	36.0
Total	62.0	5.5	67.5	23.5	9.0	32.5	100.0

MARITAL STATUS

Marital status or marital structure is an important aspect of occupational studies as it tends to affect the mobility and participation in the work-force. Marriages in India are almost universal and it is also evident from our sample (Table 4.3), that more than 85 per cent of respondents are married. Among unmarried librarians, the percentage of women is somewhat higher as compared to men. It should not be surprising given the fact that the proportion of unmarried females in urban areas is 29.2 per cent.[12] When marital status is viewed age-wise, we find that more than half of the unmarried women are concentrated in the young age, and hence, it is expected that most of them may get married in due course of time, as the mean age of marriage for educated women is 22.07. However, a small section of them may become the victim of higher education and family obligation. So far as the young unmarried males are concerned, they have certainly better chances for getting married.

RELIGION

Religion, caste and language are the important dimensions of Indian social structure. Religion brings homogeneity in regard to practice and way of life. Apart from the influence that it exerts on the thought and socialisation of the people, it also justifies the caste system and consequently regulates interpersonal and intergroup relations.[13] Now with the adoption of secular values in our society, neither religion nor caste has any legal basis in barring an individual for taking up any occupation. But in actual practice certain pre-entry qualifications prescribed by modern occupations may not be easily available to the members of the traditionally disadvantage groups for taking up such occupations.

Data regarding the religious background of respondents have been presented in Table 4.4. Along with the representation of various religious communities in the sample, their proportions in the population of Delhi and in India have also been provided for the purpose of comparison.

The preponderence of Hindus in Indian society is well reflected in the sample. The more or less proportionate representation of majority religion (87.5 per cent) is quite understandable, as we see the same trend in most of the empirical studies of professions conducted in Delhi. In the case of medical profession, Oommen[14] noticed that 85.8 per cent of doctors were Hindus, and Madan[15] found 84 per cent in his sample. In the study of college teachers of Delhi, Bali[16] identified that as large as 89.44 per cent of teachers were from Hindu community. Besides Hindus, a small number of librarians were also drawn from Muslim, Sikh and Christian communities.

TABLE 4.4: **Distribution of Respondents by their Religions along with Comparative Figures of Various Religious Groups in India and in Delhi (Percentage)**

Religious groups	Distribution in the sample		Distribution in Delhi (1981 Census)	Distribution in India (1981 Census)
	Frequency	%	%	%
Hindus	175	87.5	83.60	83.64
Muslims	12	6.0	7.74	11.35
Sikhs	10	5.0	6.33	1.96
Other religious groups	3	1.5	2.33	3.05
Total	200	100.0	100.0	100.0

CASTE

Caste is said to be a unique feature of Indian society. It was the traditional system of stratification which worked as the mechanism for the allocation of persons for different occupations. With the introduction of English education, the traditional function of castes has changed, as Ghurye observes:

> the caste no longer rigidly determines individuals' occupations, but continues to prescribe almost in its old rigour the circle into which one has to marry. But change in the economic conditions have led many castes to clamour for petty jobs in the clerical lines.[17]

In the changed circumstances, none of the castes have any legitimate claim over any modern occupation. Therefore, it would be interesting to know how far the different caste categories are represented in modern occupation such as the librarianship.

Data regarding the caste background of respondents were analysed in the case of Hindu librarians only, who were 175 in number as mentioned in Table 4.4 in the proceeding section. Of the total Hindu librarians, 27 did not reveal their caste identity. However, this shows their negative attitude towards the caste system. Thus, our final analysis in this regard is based on the caste identification of 148 respondents. For ordering the information about the specific castes of respondents, we adopted three-fold classification: (i) the three twice born varanas, Brahmin, Kshatriya, and Vaishya, including Khattri and Kayastha, (ii) the intermediary castes, which are not twice born, such as jat, goldsmith, etc., and (iii) the Scheduled Castes.

It is significant to note that the majority of respondents (66.2 per cent) are mainly from three twice-born varãnas; the representation of respondents from intermediary castes is confined only 23.6 per cent and the rest 10.2 per cent belongs to lower castes.

The question as to why the highest percentage of respondents hailed from upper caste is sociologically relevant. In this regard, one of the reasons could be that a certain level of socio-economic development, which is a necessary pre-requisite to gain entry into the profession, is available to a greater extent, to upper castes only. The situation, as analysed by Srinivas, points out:

> In urban areas, the Brahmins were the first to sense the advantage of Western education and sons of those who left the village became the first teachers, lawyers, doctors and judges. Their position in the social system was strategic in the rural areas and they constituted the regions and landed aristrocracy, in urban area they had a near monopoly of all the higher posts.[18]

Thus the low representation of members of intermediary and lower castes may seem to be the consequence of their social and educational backwardness. Realising the existence of socio-economic disparities in such communities, the provisions were made in the Indian Constitution to provide them with some ameliorative measures for raising their standards in the social strata.

According to the Census of India, 1981, the Scheduled Castes approximately constitute 18.03 per cent of Delhi's population and 15.75 per cent of India's population. The enrolment figures for the Scheduled Castes in higher educational courses suggest that they constitute 7.36 per cent in the region of Delhi.[19] The policy of reservation pursued by the Government of India has evidently shown encouraging impact, judging from the 10.2 per cent Scheduled Castes representation in library profession.

Besides librarianship, it would be worthwhile to examine the representation of Scheduled Castes in other professions too. Gore et al.,[20] in their survey of school teachers in India, reported that while teachers from Scheduled Castes would not average more than 5 per cent, in two States there were no Scheduled Caste teachers at all. Compared to librarianship and teaching, the representation of Scheduled Castes in other prestigious professions like medicine was found nearly nil. Madan[21] in his study of medical profession in Delhi and Ghaziabad did not find any doctor from the population of Scheduled Castes. In a similar study, Oommen[22] noticed the total absence of house surgeons and nurses from Scheduled Castes. However, Dubey[23] noticed the negligible percentage of Scheduled Castes (2.66 per cent) in his study of five professions in Gorakhpur. In a recent study of college teachers in Delhi, the population of Scheduled Caste teachers in colleges was stated to be just 0.65 per cent.[24] It seems that in spite of the ameliorative measures provided to the lower castes, they have not improved their entry into the prestigious professions, like medicine, engineering and college teaching. On the other hand, as the entry qualifications in librarianship and school teaching are less competitive, their representation in these professions is better.

An analysis of the caste data in relation to sex, indicates that the women librarians were mainly from upper castes and only a small percentage of them (17 per cent) belonged to intermediary and lower castes. It is clear that the acceptability of women's education has not gained sufficient ground among intermediary and lower caste categories. Further it also reveals that the educational gains and other facilities are mostly utilised by the male members of these castes, as it is evident that low caste female librarians constitute only 22 per cent of the total low caste male librarians. This situation is also closely related to low literacy rates among lower caste females. Thus, it seems that the traditional attitude towards females is more persistent among lower caste people.

LINGUISTIC-REGIONAL BACKGROUND

Cultural diversity and multi-lingualism are the distinctive features of Indian society. The Census of India, 1971, lists as many as 1652 mother tongues. Schedule VIII of the Indian Constitution had recognised 15 Indian languages for official use in the State administration.[25] As much as 95.4 per cent of the population claim one of these languages as their mother-tongue. Hindi is the language of 38 per cent of the population. After Hindi, Bengali and Telugu come next in importance. Delhi, being the capital city of India, has the distinction of representing most of the linguistic groups in its region. Interestingly, our sample also represents almost all the major languages mentioned in the

Constitution.

The language-wise distribution of respondents has been presented in Table 4.5. It may be seen that 53 per cent of respondents are the Hindi-speaking people who are under represented in comparison to their proportion in the population of Delhi (75.97). On the other hand, Punjabis are having disproportionate representation. Similarly, the representation of Bengalis is also somewhat higher in the sample.

TABLE 4.5: **Distribution of Respondents by their Sex and Language Background (Percentage)**

Language group	Sex (N=200)		Total	Distribution of language groups in the population of Delhi according to Census 1971 (%-wise)
	Male	Female		
Hindi	58.5	41.5	53.0	75.97
Punjabi	15.6	40.0	23.5	13.40
Urdu	7.4	3.1	6.0	5.68
Bengali	5.2	4.6	5.0	1.01
Other Languages	13.3	10.8	12.5	3.94
Total (All Groups)	100.00	100.0	100.0	100.0

An almost approximate representation of Urdu knowing people seems to be merely a coincidence. Other respondents who speak Tamil, Telugu, Kannada, Malayalam, Marathi, Gujarati, Sindhi, Oriya and Kashmiri constitute one-tenth of the total sample. These groups were included in the "other languages" (Table 4.5).

The wide representation of various linguistic groups in the library profession seems to be an important feature. Apparently it indicates that the profession is more open in respect of linguistic representation. The reason for their openness has some relation with the policy of selection also. Professional librarians having additional knowledge of regional or foreign languages get preferential treatment in the recruitment, because their language skills are needed for the treatment of multi-lingual reading materials and for dealing with various linguistic groups.

In the case of Punjabi speaking group, we have earlier noted that they have disproportionate representation in the library profession. The sex-wise distribution of respondents in the same language group further reveals that as compared to Punjabi men librarians (15.6 per cent) the percentage of Punjabi women librarians (40.0 per cent) is strikingly higher. Obviously it seems that in the Punjabi families library education is considered more suitable for girls rather than boys.

REGIONAL BACKGROUND

In India with the exception of few languages (e.g. Urdu) almost each major language has a territorial anchorage. According to Schedule VIII of the Constitution of India, more than 75 per cent of the speakers of each of the 15 languages are concentrated in one particular State or another. The natural concentration of various linguistic groups in the States leads to the ideology of "localism" and claims of the "sons of the soil" in services and enterprises there.

However, the case of Delhi is different; being the capital city, all linguistic groups are supposed to have equal claim here, what is also confirmed by our data. As we have noticed earlier that Delhi shows an unique pattern in matters of library development. With the growth of various national level centres or institutions in Delhi it is expected that most of the professionals would move out from their native States in search of better career opportunities. On the other hand, there is also a general tendency that for a number of reasons only a limited proportion of the people move out from their place of origin. In our study respondents were asked to identify the regions to which they belonged to. The analysis indicated the inter-regional mobility as well as the regional background of the library professionals.

It is clear from Table 4.6 that respondents are pre-dominantly (88 per cent) from north India and half of them are from Delhi alone. In other words, with the exception of 2.5 per cent of respondents who belong to Kashmir, all the respondents from north India belong to Hindi or Punjabi speaking groups. Among the neighbouring States of Delhi, Uttar Pradesh accounts for highest inter-regional mobility. Besides Punjab and Kashmir, the librarians from other non-Hindi States (Tamil Nadu, Karnataka, Kerala, West Bengal, Orissa, Maharashtra and Gujarat) constitute only 12 per cent. In the case of Bengalis it was revealed that the father of only one Bengali respondent was inhabitant of Delhi while others were migrants from West Bengal. Of total librarians in our sample, 42 per cent of them belong to Delhi while 58 per cent of them are first generation migrants. This shows a substantial inter-regional mobility among librarians.

TABLE 4.6: **Distribution of Respondents by their Sex and Regional Background (in percentage)**

Regional Background	Sex (N = 200)		Total
	Male (N = 135)	Female (N = 65)	
Delhi	34.8	69.2	46.0
Northern Region	51.1	23.1	42.0
Uttar Pradesh	25.9	9.2	20.5
Haryana	11.9	1.5	8.5
Madhya Pradesh	3.0	00.0	2.0
Punjab	4.4	4.6	4.5
Rajasthan	3.7	3.1	3.5
Jammu & Kashmir	1.5	4.6	2.5
Himachal Pradesh	0.7	0.0	0.5
Southern Region	3.7	1.5	3.0
Eastern Region	6.0	3.1	5.0
Western Region	4.4	3.1	4.0
Total	100.0	100.0	100.0

In the context of inter-regional mobility, men and women librarians show opposite trends. Out of the total librarians in our sample, 65.2 per cent men are from outside States, while less than one-third of women librarians are migrants from other States. It may also be noted that the neighbouring State Utter Pradesh accounts for one-third of the total migration of the women librarians. Understandably, in the case of women professionals the location of their husbands' jobs, their familial responsibility and blocked aspirations for their own careers act as restrictive factors for their mobility.

The regional characteristic of librarians, as reflected in this study, seems to be in conformity with the finding of other professional groups studied in Delhi region. In the study of college teachers of Delhi[26] it was revealed that 46.83 per cent of teachers were from other non-Hindi States. Even such organisation as the All India Institute of Medical Sciences did not have more than 20 per cent of their faculty from non-Hindi States.[27] In the case of other cosmopolitan hospitals in Delhi, it was found that as many as 74.8 per cent of doctors were mainly from north India.[28]

RURAL-URBAN BACKGROUND

The rural-urban background of individuals tends to influence their educational and occupational achievements. It may also influence their social values and attitudes. The various studies of professional groups demonstrate the urban origin of their members. It is a general trend that modern professions are monopolised by the urbanites. This is so because the facilities to acquire the prerequisites for modern professions such as formal education, credentials and regular training for a prescribed period, are largely concentrated in urban agglomerations. So the urbanites are in a better position to equip themselves with modern knowledge and skill which later on facilitate their entry into professions. The facilities for professional education in librarianship are available mainly in big cities and capital towns. Therefore, it is not surprising that the library professionals with urban background predominate in the profession. But in order to ascertain the trend more specifically, we asked the respondents to report about the place where they had spent the first fifteen years of their life. The distinction between city and town was left to the judgement of the respondents.

As expected, majority of respondents (75.5 per cent) had an urban or semi-urban upbringing. The respondents who had rural upbringing constituted 24.5 per cent. However, with the exception of one lady who had rural background, the rest grew up in urban environment. Needless to mention that rural parents have many constraints in sending their daughters to urban areas for higher education or professional education. This explains the relatively low representation of women from rural sector in the library profession.

FAMILY BACKGROUND

In order to understand the family background of librarians, we selected three aspects, viz., education, occupation, and economic status, of their fathers. In Indian families, fathers perform a crucial role and they are the major determinant of the familial status. The study of educational and occupational achievements of their fathers would help us in understanding the course of social change and direction of inter-generation educational mobility.

Studies in the field of occupational mobility demonstrated the role of formal education in occupational change. Gist[29] indicated that the changes in the traditional occupations in South India were brought out by the system of Western education. Similarly both Lambert[30] and Driver[31] in their independent studies noticed the positive impact of education on social mobility.

Given the educational background of respondents who usually had post-graduate education, educational levels of their fathers would serve to indicate the inter-generational educational mobility.

TABLE 4.7: **Distribution of Respondents by their Sex and Fathers' Education (%)**

Levels of Education of Respondents' fathers	Sex (N = 200)		
	Male (N = 135)	Female (N = 65)	Total
Illiterate	6.7	3.0	5.5
Literate without formal education	5.9	6.1	6.0
Below matriculation	24.4	12.3	20.5
Matriculation and below graduation	30.4	21.6	27.5
Graduation	24.4	33.9	27.5
Post-Graduation/Professional and Technical education	8.2	23.1	13.0
	100.0	100.0	100.0

The educational background of respondents' fathers as categorised in Table 4.7 may be grouped mainly into three categories for better comprehension. Thus, we find that 40.5 per cent of respondents' fathers were graduates, 27.5 per cent were matriculates and the rest 32 per cent of them had education below high school level.

The fathers of women librarians were better educated than the fathers of men librarians. The data reveal that 57 per cent of the fathers of female librarians were graduates as against a corresponding figure of 32.6 per cent. Thirty-seven per cent of the fathers of gents librarians were non-matriculates as against 21.4 per cent of fathers of women librarians.

It was found that fathers of librarians from lower castes were all illiterate or were educated below matriculation. In the case of librarians from intermediate castes, we found that 48 per cent of their fathers had also the same level of education. The close relationship between caste and education thus seems to be evident. To sum up, librarians are an educationally upward mobile group. The overwhelming majority, 73.5 per cent of librarians were more educated than their fathers, 21 per cent equally educated and only 5.5 per cent less educated.

OCCUPATIONAL STATUS OF FATHERS

Information regarding specific occupations of the fathers of respondents were grouped in the following categories: super-administrative services; subordinate administrative and ministerial services; professions such as law, medicine, teaching, etc.; agriculture; business and 'others' — the last category was to include those occupations which were of non-specific types.

Nearly 30 per cent (29.5 per cent) of the fathers of respondents were in the subordinate administrative and ministerial services and only 10 per cent (9.5 per cent) of the librarians claimed that their fathers had high administrative jobs. The sons of lawyers, doctors, university and school teachers, who joined librarianship constituted nearly 15 per cent (14.5 per cent). Eighteen per cent were in agriculture, 19.0 per cent in business and the remaining 9.5 per cent were in 'other' occupations.

The above distribution of the occupations of the fathers of respondents clearly indicates that the recruitment in the librarianship is mainly from urban occupations — which shows only inter-stratum mobility. The mobility between the strata accounts for only 37 per cent. In a set of urban occupations, white-collar groups alone supply as much as 40 per cent of the librarians and the contribution of the urban professional classes accounts for less than 15 per cent. Thus, considering the dominance of urban groups in librarianship, it seems to be more biased towards the sons and daughters of men of lower administrative services than that of higher administrative services and professional classes. This is so because the urban upper or upper middle class aspire to be in more prestigious occupations. Evidently the vast agricultural population contributes only few librarians (18.0 per cent). Since library education and development are concentrated in urban agglomerations, the above trend does not seem to be contradictory.

SUBJECTIVE PERCEPTIONS OF ECONOMIC STATUS

Having known educational and occupational backgrounds of the fathers of respondents, it is important to ascertain their parental economic status. It may be stated that the evaluation of economic status of their fathers was based on their perceptions of incomes of their fathers, depending upon their own experiences of social milieu. Categories of economic status suggested to the respondents were: high or 'well-off', average, low or 'difficult'.

Surprisingly only a negligible percentage (3.5 per cent) of respondents considered their fathers to be economically well-off. The majority of librarians (68.5 per cent) were brought up in the average economic conditions; 28 per cent of them had difficult economic backgrounds.

It is evident that the overwhelming majority of librarians were recruited from the lower middle or lower strata of the society. The data revealed that more male librarians (29.6 per cent) belonged to low economic strata than their female counterparts (18.5 per cent). The lower economic background of librarians was further corroborated by a study[32] of students seeking admissions in Library and Information Science education. The study reflected that majority of (56.66 per cent) students belonged to middle income group and 23.33 per cent belonged to low income group. Number of students who hailed from high income group was comparatively less, i.e., 20 per cent.

The recruitment base of librarians indicates more similarity with school teachers. Gore et al.,[33] in their study indicated that the largest category of teachers belonged to average circumstances and the next largest group of men teachers came from 'difficult' or 'stringent' circumstances. Interestingly, the study also revealed that the percentages of male school teachers from 'well-off' circumstances varied between three to six per cent. In a study of Delhi school teachers,[34] it was found that male teachers were recruited from rural lower economic levels. Contrary to the librarians and secondary school teachers, a sizeable number of doctors[35] (36.5 per cent) were from well-off families and only 3.3 per cent of them had difficult economic conditions.

EDUCATIONAL AND PROFESSIONAL ATTAINMENTS

While not minimising the role of socio-cultural and economic factors in shaping life style of individuals, it is really the type of education and training which help them in choosing a particular vocation or profession. The professions, in particular, provide opportunities to them for the growth of further knowledge and skill, which in turn help them in career progression, in and outside the organisation. In any library organisation, apart from the professionally trained librarians, there are para-professionals and ministerial staff. It is expected that some of these categories of staff can, in due course, acquire higher academic and professional qualifications and aspire to climb the ladder of professional positions through the prevalent promotional channel or through competitive means. Similarly, the professional librarians can also try to gain higher academic and professional qualifications in order to get more senior positions in organisations. Therefore, it would be pertinent to enquire about educational and professional attainments of the respondents which would reveal the intrageneration educational mobility among them.

It may be recalled that the minimum educational and professional requirements for becoming a professional librarian in India are a Bachelor degree in any discipline and a Bachelor degree in Library and Information Science. Evidently, a comparison of educational and professional achievements of the respondents at the time of their first entry into the profession with that of their present levels of achievements would indicate the direction of intragenerational educational mobility among them.

Respondents may be grouped into three categories in respect of their academic achievements: Undergraduate, graduate and post-graduate. While more than half of the respondents (54.0 per cent) were post-graduates at the time of entry into the profession, a sizeable proportion of them (38.0 per cent) possessed only the minimum educational qualification (i.e., graduation). However, 8 per cent of them had only under-graduate education. It was revealed that respondents who had only undergraduate education were men from low income rural families whereas majority of the respondents who had post-graduate education belonged to well-off families.

Viewing the present academic qualifications of the respondents we find that overwhelming majority of them (80 per cent) have post-graduate degrees while only 20 per cent of them are graduates. Comparing the qualifications of respondents which they had at the time of entry along with their present ones, we find that 46 per cent of them achieved academic excellence after joining the profession.

In respect of professional qualifications, we find that 18 per cent of the respondents joined the profession without having any requisite professional qualification. Respondents who had only minimum level of professional qualification (*i.e.*, Bachelor's degree in Library and

Information Science) constituted 65 per cent. There were only 17 per cent of respondents who had higher level of professional degree (*i.e.*, Master's degree in Library and Information Science or Associateship in Documentation) when they had joined the profession. At present 62 per cent of them have minimum level of professional degrees and the remaining 38 per cent have higher professional qualifications. Thus, we find that more than one-third of respondents (36 per cent) had advanced their professional knowledge by acquiring degrees while remaining in the job.

LEVELS OF PROFICIENCY

Levels of proficiency achieved by the respondents in their academic careers may be seen in terms of their performance in various examinations. In their matriculation examinations, 13.5 per cent of respondents had first divisions, 68.5 per cent had second divisions and the remaining 18.0 per cent of them got third divisions. At the graduation level, less than sixty per cent (56.5 per cent) of them had second class while a sizeable group (38.0 per cent) obtained third class. The respondents who achieved first class constituted a negligible percentage (5.5 per cent). However, they performed better at the master level. While only 7.8 per cent of librarians had first class, the majority of them (67.6 per cent) had second class; and the remaining one fourth of them (24.6 per cent) were placed in the third class.

It is possible to make a comparison of the academic achievements of the librarians at the master level with that of the college teachers, as we have some data in this regard. Chitnis[36] in the case of teachers of Bombay reported that 35 per cent of them had a first class career, 58 per cent had a second class career and 7 per cent had a third class career. Evidently the majority of librarians have moderate academic career as compared to the teachers.

In the case of librarians we also observe that more than one-third of respondents (35 per cent) had irregular academic careers. Twwnty-two per cent of them took as long as five to seven years to secure a Master's degree and the remaining 13 per cent took four years. However, it is satisfying to note that respondents had better performances in professional examinations. More than one-fourth of respondents obtained first class in the Bachelor's degree in Library and Information Science and less than 15 per cent of them obtained first class in the Master's degree.

ORGANISATIONAL ATTRIBUTES

Besides studying the personal attributes, socio-economic background, educational and professional achievements of respondents, there is need to know how librarians are resocialised by their organisations. This is because their routes of entry into the profession, their ranks, and experiences in organisations may likely to influence their role-perceptions, role-commitments, and their bureaucratic and professional behaviour.

(a) Type of Libraries

In our sample 41.5 per cent of librarians were drawn from university libraries, 42 per cent were from special libraries and the remaining 16.5 per cent were from public libraries. In order to understand how professionals are inducted into different types of libraries, we asked them to provide information about their careers in various organisations. Data regarding the first entry of initial recruitment of librarians in various types of libraries were analysed. It was found that from the 44 per cent of them who joined academic libraries, 34 per cent entered into the university libraries and 10 per cent got their appointments in college libraries. 46.5 per cent of respondents started their career in special libraries and only 9.5 per cent of them joined public libraries. It is clear that public library system is not yet properly developed to attract sufficient number of professionals as compared to special and university libraries.

(b) Recruitment

There are two routes of entry into the library profession. While a great majority of respondents (75 per cent) were recruited into professional positions in the different types of libraries, it is also significant to note that one-fourth of them (25 per cent) took non-professional or para-professional routes of entry into the profession. That is to say, they did not start first career as professional librarians but were appointed as clerks, library attendants, library assistants etc. in the libraries. In due course of time, while remaining in the jobs, they acquired both academic and professional qualifications and obtained the professional positions through promotion channel or through open competition.

(c) **Rand of Professionals in Libraries**

There are wide variations in the designations and pay-scales of librarians in various types of libraries. Based on their designations and salary-structure, we categorised them into three hierarchical levels, viz., senior, middle and junior.

Of the total sample of librarians, 47 per cent of them were in the junior levels, 40 per cent were in the middle levels and 13 per cent were in the senior levels. The sex-wise distribution of respondents according to their organisational levels, revealed that 36.4 per cent of men and 69.2 per cent of women were in the junior levels; 45.9 per cent of men and 27.7 per cent of women were in the middle levels and 17.7 per cent of males and 3.1 per cent of women were in the senior levels. It is obvious that majority of women (69.2 per cent) were in junior levels while majority of men (63.6 per cent) were in middle and senior levels. As explained earlier, since women's entry in the profession is relatively recent, their lower percentage in the middle and senior levels is not unexpected.

When age-groups of respondents were viewed rank-wise, it was found that a great majority (72.9 per cent) of young (age between 25 to 34 years) professionals were in the junior levels and only 27.1 per cent of them were placed in the middle ranks. It seems to be unlikely that a person in young age would climb to senior positions in the libraries. Even in the case of middle-aged professionals (age between 35 and 44 years) only a negligible percentage of them (8.7 per cent) were in the senior rank. Consequently middle ranks were dominated by young (49.3 per cent) and middle-aged (42.0 per cent) professionals. As for the professionals in higher age group, 48.6 per cent of them were placed in the middle levels, 27.8 per cent in senior levels, and the remaining 23.6 per cent were still working at junior levels.

(d) **Professional Experience**

In formal organisations, very often, experience or seniority plays an important role in deciding one's promotion or enhancement other than the merit. In the case of libraries, senior positions are mostly given to professionals sufficiently experienced and in addition, satisfying other requirements. While no experience may be needed for offering most junior positions in libraries, professionals having good experiences are generally recruited on the middle level positions.

For the purpose of convenience, respondents were categorised into four groups on the basis of their experiences; up to 5 years, 6 to 10 years, 11 to 20 years and having experience more than 21 years. Out of total respondents, 18 per cent had up to 5 years of experience, 24 per cent had 6 to 10 years of experience, 36.5 per cent had 11 to 20 years of experience and 21.5 per cent had more than 21 years of experience. It may be noted that the respondents' categorisation, on the basis of their experiences, more or less coincides with their hierarchical levels.

To sum up, we have made an attempt to describe the personal attributes, the social background, educational and professional attainments and organisational attributes of 200 librarians who responded to our questionnaires. It should be emphasised here that our intention was to know certain salient features of respondents assuming that some of these may influence their career patterns, their role perception and their bureaucratic and professional orientations, which are be considered in the subsequent chapters.

NOTES

1. Mary Biggs (1982), "Librarians and the 'Woman questions': An Enquiry into the Conservatism", *Journal of Library History*, Vol. 17, pp. 409-28.
2. Paul D. Montagna (1977), *Towards a Sociology of the Labour Market*, London: John Wiley, pp. 129-30.
3. Richard L. Simpson and Ida Harper Simpson (1969), "Women and Bureaucracy in the Semi-Professions", in Amitai Etzioni (ed.), *The Semi Professions and Their Organisations*, London, The Free Press, pp. 196-247.
4. Anita R. Schiller (1974), "Women in Librarianship" in Melvin J. Voigt (ed.), *Advances in Librarianship*, New York, Academic Press, pp. 104-47.
5. *Ibid.*
6. John P. Robinson, Robert Athanasiou and Kendra B. Head (1969), *Measures of Occupational Characteristics*, Ann Arbor, Michigan: University of Michigan Survey Research Centre, Institute for Social Research, p. 438.
7. *Census of India, 1981, Series-1, India, Part II, Special* (Reports and Tables based on 5 per cent Sample Data), Delhi: Registrar General and Census Commissioner for India, 1983.
8. *Census of India, 1971, Series 27, Delhi, Part II-B, General Economic Tables*, Delhi: Director of Census Operations, 1981.
9. *Census of India, 1981, Series 28, Delhi, Part III-A&B and Part IV-A*, Delhi: Director of Census Operations, 1981.
10. The DHTP Survey was conducted in 1981 along with population census by the Division for Scientific Technical Personnel of the Council of Scientific and Industrial Research (CSIR), New Delhi. *See Degree Holders and Technical Personnel Survey : Census 1981, Statistical Tables on Social Sciences, Arts, Humanities*

and Commerce, Vol. I p. xiv. New Delhi, Council of Scientific and Industrial Research, Division for Scientific and Technical Personnel, 1990.

11. India, Status of Women in India (Report of the Committee on —), *Towards Equality*, New Delhi: Ministry of Education and Social Welfare, 1971.
12. Ashish Bose (1975), "A Demographic Profile of Indian Women", in Devaki Jain (ed.), *Indian Women*, New Delhi: Publications Division, Ministry of Information and Broadcasting.
13. Richard F. Nyrop (1957), et al., *Area Handbook for India*, Washington, D.C., The American University, p. 157.
14. T.K. Oommen (1978), *Doctors and Nurses: A Study in Occupational Role Structures*. Delhi: Macmillan, p. 44.
15. T.N. Madna (1980), "India: Doctors at the All India Institute of Medical Sciences", T.N. Madan et al., *Doctors and Society: Three Asian Case Studies, India, Malaysia and Sri Lanka*, Ghaziabad: Vikas, p. 50.
16. Arun P. Bali (1986), *College Teachers: Challenges and Response*, New Delhi: Northern Book Centre, p. 69
17. G.S. Ghurye (1961), *Caste, Class and Occupation*, Bombay: Popular Prakashan, p. 209.
18. M.N. Srinivas (1962), *Caste in Modern India*, Bombay: Asia Publishing House, p. 86.
19. University Grants Commission (1985), *Facilities to Scheduled Castes and Scheduled Tribes in University and Colleges* (Analysis on the position of actual admissions and employment of Scheduled Castes and Scheduled Tribes in universities and colleges during 1978-79), New Delhi: UGC, p. 70.
20. M.S. Gore, I.P. Desai and Suma Chitnis (1974), "School Teachers in India: Findings of All India Study in Sociology of Education", in Satya Pal Ruhela (ed.), *Sociology of the Teaching Profession in India*, New Delhi, National Council of Educational Research and Training, pp. 83-122.
21. T.N. Madan (1980), op. cit., p. 51.
22. T.K. Oommen (1978), op. cit., p. 46.
23. S.M. Dubey (1973), *Social Mobility Among the Professions: Study of the Professions in a Transitional Indian Society*, Bombay: Popular Prakashan, p. 64.
24. Arun P. Bali (1986), op. cit., p. 70.
25. Mangal Chandra Jain Kagzi (1984), *The Constitution of India*, 2 Vols., Vol. I (ed. 4), Delhi: Metropolitan Book Co., pp. 160-61.
26. Arun P. Bali (1986), op. cit., p. 69.
27. T.N. Madan (1980), op. cit., p. 53.
28. T.K. Oommen (1978), op. cit., p. 49.
29. Noel Gist (1954), "Caste Differentials in South India", *American Sociological Review*, Vol. 19, pp. 130-34.
30. R.D. Lambert (1963), *Workers, Factories and Social Change in India*, Princeton: Asia Publishing House and the Gokhale Institute of Politics and Economics, pp. 162-65.
31. Edwin D. Driver (1962), "Caste and Occupational Structure in Central India", *Social Forces*, Vol. 41, pp. 26-36.
32. G. Devarajan (1983), "Admission Seeking Variables in Library and Information Science Students: A Socio-Economic Profile", *ALIS Bulletin*, Vol. 7, pp. 37-41.
33. M.S. Gore, I.P. Desai and Suma Chitnis (1970), "School Teachers in India: Find-

ings of an All India Study in Sociology of Education", in Satya Pal Ruhela (ed.), *Sociology of the Teaching Profession in India*, New Delhi: National Council of Educational Research and Training, pp. 101-103.

34. Satya Pal Ruhela (1970), "Professionalisation of School Teachers in India", op. cit.
35. T.K. Oommen (1978), op. cit., p. 57.
36. Suma Chitnis (1979), "College Teachers: Constraints to Professionalisation", in Suma Chitnis and P. G. Altbach (eds.), *The Indian Academic Profession*, Delhi: Macmillan.

FIVE

OCCUPATIONAL CAREER OF LIBRARIANS

FOR THE analysis of occupational career of a professional group, it is important to ask why an individual member embarks upon a particular profession and when he enters into it what factors motive him to remain in that occupation. But after one's entry into an occupation, his commitment for that occupation would largely depend upon the extrinsic rewards which he would likely to derive from his occupation; the status or prestige which would be accorded to him in lieu of his service to the society and the extent of satisfaction which he would get from his career.

OCCUPATIONAL CHOICE

The decision to choose an occupation has important implications both for an individual and for his society. When an individual selects an occupation he at once commits himself to a certain pattern of thought and behaviour which tends to affect his entire personality. As work in every society is graded according to its skill, knowledge, creativity, and values, a person selects an occupation which would provide him the opportunities for his self-fulfilment, self-actualisation, creativity and productivity. Studies on occupational choice suggest that people who enter different occupations have different outlooks on work 'as a fact of life'. Rosenberg[1] and his associates contend that people who enter different kinds of occupations have basically different values. According to Schwarzweller,[2] values are social facts which ultimately influence the structure and organisation of labour market. In his study on occupational value orientations, he ascertained the relationship between values and the career planning situations. The twelve value variables (value on achievement, material comfort, security, hard work, creative work with people, service to society, individualism, familism, external conformity, friendship), which Schwarzweller selected for his study, represent three broad areas of meaning: (i) orientation toward ends extrinsic to the job selection situation; (ii) orientation towards ends intrinsic to the job selection situation and (iii) orientation towards ends satisfying certain moral conditions of living. His findings suggest that (a) value orientations influence occupational selection and (b) occupational value orientations are learned in the socialisation process.

Simpson and Simpson[3] studied the value and sources of personal influence in the occupational decisions of undergraduate students. In their study, they included three occupational fields such as business occupation (e.g., retail proprietor, manufacturer's representative and corporation manager or executive), scientific and aesthetic occupations (e.g., actor, commercial artist, musician, journalist, advertising, writer, doctor, scientist) and general cultural occupations (e.g., teacher, professor, lawyer, and all of those occupations which are professional or semi-professional that involve direct contact with people) which represent three different types of values. Business occupations give emphasis on extrinsic rewards (e.g., high income); scientific and aesthetic occupations are known to acquire specialised skills and provide self-expression and general cultural occupations are valued for the social contribution they make. Their findings suggest that values, personal influence and occupational choice are interrelated. It was broadly indicated that students, who were prospective businessmen, were not very interested in the self-expression through work, instead they emphasised income and leisure. On the other hand, students who were planning scientific and aesthetic careers, showed strong motivation for success within their own situation. The other types of students who were planning to enter general cultural occupations expressed their concern for contributing to social welfare through their work. Regarding the sources of influence on their careers, business-oriented students cited parental influence while students who intended to enter scientific and aesthetic occupations and general cultural occupations, were more likely to name teachers and professors.

Career in librarianship or library organisations may also be viewed as a process of enhancement of value of life. Ranganathan[4] conceptualised the possible values which library science purports. According to him, career in librarianship may be pursued for personal profit (*Swartha*), 'social well-being' (*Samuhika-Sukha*) 'creative joy' (*pramoda*), 'fulfilment of a nation's mission' (*desiya-dharma*), and 'delight (*ananda*). Ranganathan's conceptualisation of these five values are in conformity with the Indian tradition of fundamental values of life (*purususharthas*), *Dharma*, *Artha*, *Kama* and *Moksha*. He considered 'personal profit' in the category of *artha* (wealth). The social betterment of *samuhika-sukha* belongs to the category of *Kama* or happiness in the vital plane. The two values 'creative work' (*Swiya dharma*) and 'nation's welfare' (*desiya-dharma*) combine together to serve the purpose of *dharma* which ultimately lead to *Anand* or delight. The fifth purpose for pursuing the career of librarianship relates to the attainment of *Moksha* or 'Release' which is concomitant to *Ananda*. *Moksha* provides ever-lasting delight which is the ultimate goal of librarianship. He contended that all the above five purposes can be attained equally and simultaneously, so library professional should not attempt to stop at the first value ('personal profit') but they should give undivided devotion to library science for the attainment of *Moksha* or having 'Ever-lasting Delight'.

Whatever may be the values associated with a particular occupation, tne process of occupational choice is itself viewed as a 'series of progressive delimitations of alternatives' as suggested by Rosenberg.[5] There are number of factors, e.g., individual, social and occupational, which operate to restrict the occupational possibilities of the individuals.[6] Social characteristics, which influence their entry to the occupational careers, are the level of knowledge, intelligence[7] and interest[8], their ability and education, their social position and relationship and their orientation toward occupational life. Eventually the individuals take decisions within a very limited narrow range.

Among the above characteristics, the role of family in the occupational choice is very important. It is the family which determines the financial resources for preparing the children for their occupational roles. The occupational experiences of the parents exert considerable influence on the occupational decisions of their off-springs. The elements of family structure tend to mould the personality and attitude of persons through the process of socialisation of the individuals. The process of socialisation, as we know, is not confined to the family alone, so the role of relatives, peers and teachers are equally important in influencing the attitude of individuals for educational attainment that ultimately imposes restrictions on occupational decision. Thus, educational attainment which is an "achieved characteristic" acts itself as "ascribed characteristic" like status or origin in the occupational choice.[9]

Similarly, the occupational characteristics such as job-market conditions, technical qualifications, social appropriateness of the occupation (e.g., occupations of nursing and school teaching are viewed as "female occupations") and the non-functional requirements of the occupation (e.g., reservation of jobs for a particular social category) etc. are also important determinants for occupational entry.[10]

Notwithstanding the fact that occupational choice has important implications for an individual, it is often found that a person enters the job market with limited and vague information about the occupation. Reynold's study[11] of labour market suggests that many workers who obtained certain jobs did not have sufficient information about the range of alternative opportunities to make deliberate rational choices in their careers. As such occupational choice is restricted by lack of knowledge about existing opportunities and consequently, individuals do not make conscious decisions about occupations. Since they do not have actual experience about the requirements of jobs and rewards, their decisions are often based on inadequate and haphazard knowledge of the occupation. Miller and Form[12] observe that rational occupational choice is rare and in most cases individuals make accidental entry into the occupations. Katz and Martin, in their study of career choice among nurses, suggest that occupational choice may be viewed " . . . as a series of situational decisions which individually have no rational connection with the choice of a particular occupation but, nonetheless, comprise the process of embarkation on a career".[13]

SOURCES OF COMMUNICATION FOR OCCUPATIONAL CHOICE

The above discussion on occupational choice entails an investigation into the motivating factors for the choice of a profession. But to be motivated, one should have information. Therefore, it is necessary to know the sources through which members of a community become aware of a particular profession. Usually, parents, friends and relatives (i.e., personal network), teachers and elders of the profession (i.e., occupational network) and mass media (such as newspapers, radio, television etc.), play an important role in transmitting informations about occupations one may choose. In the case of librarians also, we made an attempt to find out what particular type of networks might have influenced our respondents in choice of the profession.

Our data reveal that the family was the source of information in respect of 57.5 per cent of respondents. For the dissemination of occupational information the role of teachers and librarians was confined to 29.5 per cent of respondents. The remaining 13 per cent of them became aware of the profession through mass media. If communication through family network (57.5 per cent) and occupational network (29.5 per cent) are considered interpersonal communications we find that an overwhelming majority of respondents (87.0 per cent) entered the occupation through the influence of interpersonal information dissemination.

Responses regarding sources of communication for occupational choice were analysed with reference to a set of four background variables, such as sex, rural-urban background, caste and occupation (Table 5.1) assuming that these might tend to influence the sources of communication. It is clear from Table 5.1 that occupational network is more closed in the case of women librarians and confined to circles of family, kin and friends. In other words, the parental influence is more predominant in the case of women librarians. Regarding the dissemination of occupational information, the effectiveness of mass media seems to operate almost equally for both the sexes. Because of low educational level and being located in the rural area, the parents of rural librarians may not have enough information about modern professions, so they seem to be less effective in communicating occupational information to their children. The same may be true for parents of lower and intermediate castes librarians. On the other hand, the fathers of upper caste librarians, having higher educational level, were in advantageous position to advise their children regarding the choice of occupation. Surprisingly, it was found that not a single respondent from lower caste background became aware of librarianship from mass media. This may have important bearing on the planning of mass media activities for making them effective for the socially disadvantageous groups under the circumstances when occupational information is completely channellised in closed family circuit. It may also be seen that a sizeable member of respondents from white-collar backgrounds were recruited into librarianship on the suggestions of their parents. This may further suggest that some particular group of professionals are within easy reach of occupational information which would mainly facilitate the social mobility within the strata and not between the strata.

To sum up, the most distinguishing features of the sources of communication for occupational choice are: (a) They are direct interactional ones, i.e., Interpersonal ones; (b) the influence of mass media is negligible and (c) substantial number of librarians are influenced by personal network. It may be emphasised that the process of dissemination of information is taking place through closed personal network, which seems to be more true for the professions, like librarianship. This suggests that in the wider sense, a process of social sponsorship is in operation, limiting entry into them from a small section of the society.

TABLE 5.1: **Sources of Communication for Occupational Choice by Background Characteristics (%)**

Background of Librarians	Source			Total
	Personal network	Occupational network	Mass media	
Sex				
Male (N=135)	52.6	34.1	13.3	100.0
Female (N=65)	67.7	20.0	12.3	100.0
Rural (N=49)	53.1	34.7	12.2	100.0
Urban (N=145)	60.0	26.9	13.1	100.0
Caste				
Upper (N=98)	63.3	26.5	10.2	100.0
Intermediate (N=30)	40.0	36.7	23.3	100.0
Lower (N=20)	60.0	40.0	0.0	100.0
Parental Occupation				
Superior and Subordinate administrative jobs (N=78)	64.1	21.8	14.1	100.0
Profession (N=29)	51.8	31.0	17.2	100.0
Agriculture (N=36)	50.0	38.9	11.1	100.0
Business (N=37)	54.1	35.1	10.8	100.0

The above observation seem to be closely associated with the sources of communication through which doctors were influenced in their choice of careers, as evident by the studies conducted by Oommen[14] and Chandani[15] independently. Chandani[16] found that parents, relatives and friends were the major sources in the occupational entry of doctors in Jodhpur. Similarly in the case of doctors of Delhi, Oommen[17] indicated that an overwhelming majority of doctors (67 per cent) and nearly half the nurses (49 per cent) were influenced by personal network in choosing their occupational career. He also noticed that the influence of mass media was negligible, and only 8 per cent doctors and 11.0 per cent nurses were influenced by occupational network.

MOTIVATIONAL ORIENTATIONS FOR THE CHOICE OF OCCUPATION

In order to understand the motivation of librarians for choosing the profession, we asked them to indicate three reasons, in order of preference, which motivated them to choose their careers. Reasons suggested by them reveal various orientations of motivation. Responses were grouped into five broad orientations: pragmatic, altruistic, self-orientation, academic and accidental or chance entry. Items included for revealing pragmatic orientations are: (a) easy to get a job; (b) inadequate finance to pursue more expensive education; (c) better prospect; and (d) easy to get admission. Altruistic motive or service-orientation which is considered as one of the core characteristics of the profession is expressed through responses, such as 'desire to serve the readers', and 'the profession offers an opportunity to spread knowledge in the society'. The academic consideration for choosing the career is revealed through responses like 'love for books' and 'desire to gain more knowledge'. Similarly, the consideration of psychological or personality factors behind choosing one's vocation or profession may not be also irrelevant. The reason being that the conception of a particular profession may be formed at the early stage of childhood and the same may influence one's choice of profession. Likewise, some individuals may opt for a particular career because of their own personality characteristics. In order to indicate the influence of personality factors in the occupational choice, items like 'to fulfil the childhood ambition' and 'calm, quite and easy going job' have been included in the questionnaire. These responses mentioned above have been labelled as 'self-orientation'. Besides these, occasionally people may undergo professional training without any pre-conceived notion or any serious considerations. They may adopt any vocation or occupation ''by accident' or 'by chance'.

As stated above, respondents were asked to check three reasons, in order of priority, for joining the profession. It was found that while all the respondents gave their first reason, their answers to the second and third preferences were limited up to 65 per cent and 47.5 per cent respectively. Therefore, our analysis in this respect is based on their first preference only. It was revealed that 31.5 per cent of respondents had 'chance entry' into the profession and 30 per cent of them had pragmatic orientations for joining the profession. Respondents who stated academic interests behind taking up librarianship constitute only 25.5 per cent. Surprisingly, only a negligible percentage of respondents (9 per cent) had altruistic motive in choosing the career of librarianship. Similarly, only four per cent of them thought that the profession would fulfil their ambitions and would be suited to their temperament.

It is important to note that almost one-third of respondents (31.5 per cent) drifted into librarianship without any definite consideration. Slater[18] found the same situation in the case of British librarians. He noticed that at least 45 per cent of librarians "were so unmotivated that they either drifted into the job by chance or default or accepted other people's verdict about what they should do with their working lives". Sergean[19] in his manpower study, also found a large group of unmotivated people in the profession. One of the reasons for having unmotivated persons in the profession could probably be due to delayed decisions on the part of professionals for the choice of occupation. In our case, it was found that more than one-fourth of respondents (26 per cent) delayed their decisions for admission into library science course by three to seven years after obtaining their graduation or master degrees. In this respect, it is also significant to note that more than half of the respondents (51.5 per cent) tried some alternative occupations before joining the librarianship. The alternative jobs which they had in the beginning of their careers were clerical, school teaching, temporary positions of teachers in the colleges, sales-representative for books and medicines, journalism etc. Regarding the past jobs held by librarians, Slater[20] also observed that "past experience of librarians was more biased to socially useful or "do-gooding" jobs and more likely to include secretarial clerical or semi-skilled or unskilled work."

Some of the respondents also reported that they had tried for various jobs wherein the recruitment is through competitive examinations. Having failed to qualify they finally came to librarianship. The reason for having 'chance entry' by respondents in the occupation could be explained in terms of possibility of lacking information about the career of librarianship at the time of their entry into higher education or while they were at the stage of graduation. In the case of accidental entry or delayed decisions, Parker has remarked, "that librarianship is a heaven for failures and misfits in other occupations".[21]

Thirty per cent of respondents deliberately joined the profession with utilitarian motive. It would not be out of place if we mention the individual items included in the category of pragmatic orientations for clear understanding. Among pragmatic orientations, 16.5 per cent of respondents thought that they could get job more easily in the libraries; 6 per cent were of the view that librarianship would provide them best opportunity for their careers, 4.5 per cent of them were forced to join the profession because of existing financial conditions of their families that would not ordinarily permit them for higher education. The remaining 3 per cent of them considered that they could get admission in library science course more easily than in other disciplines.

At this stage, it would be appropriate to quote one interesting anecdote which Ranganathan[22] mentioned at the early phase of library profession in India. The anecdote well illustrates the predominant pragmatic considerations of librarians, the parental influence on the choice of their careers; and the misconceptions which their parents had about profession:

> . . . about twenty young men taking a course in library science in a university met me. I asked them what made them choose the library career. They first said that their parents had turned them on to that career. I asked them 'Do you know the opportunities in library career' They said, 'We do not know. We have come to you just to know about them'. I asked them, 'What made your parents thrust you into the library careers without knowing its opportunities'? They gave a shocking reply. 'Our parents tell us', they said, 'that there is now much money in library career without any serious work whatsoever'. I asked, 'Are you going to be satisfied with money alone? As young men of new India, do you not require a career which will be challenge to your intellectual capacity'? Only a few of them said, 'Yes, we do want joy from intellectual work'.[23]

There is no indication that the above situation has changed considerably. In a recent study, it was disclosed that economic consideration was still predominant behind joining the library profession. 73.33 per cent of students frankly admitted that they joined the course with the intention of getting a job. They also expressed their intention to discontinue the course if they get jobs elsewhere.[24]

In librarianship, which is a service-oriented profession, like medicine and nursing, one could expect that a large number of persons would like to join the profession for fulfilling altrustic or humanitarian goals. But as our data show only a negligible percentage of respondents (9 per cent) had these goals in mind. A few respondents (4 per cent) joined the profession with the expectation that it would provide them an opportunity for self-expression.

At this stage, a comparison may be drawn between the pre-entry motivational orientations of librarians with that of any other professional group. As the data are available only about doctors and nurses from the study of Oommen,[25] so we restrict out comparison with only these two professional groups. According to the study, doctors were reported to be predominantly self-oriented and nurses were stated to be humanitarians.[26] On the contrary, we noticed that librarians had mainly pragmatic considerations or joined the profession by chance. In the case of doctors, it seems their well-off family backgrounds and achievement-ethos of their profession had motivated them towards self-orientation. Regarding nurses, it may be said that in spite of their poor economic background, they were mainly humanitarian because of the prevalent service orientation of nursing profession which might have considerably influenced their motivational orientation. But in the case of librarians, it seems their pragmatic orientations might have been anchored to their average socio-economic conditions and further strengthened by the lack of awareness of service ethos of library profession.

It is also significant to note that one-fourth (25.5 per cent) of respondents entered the profession with expectations of achieving upward educational mobility. It seems clear that many of the respondents could not continue their studies because of their poor economic conditions and they had joined the libraries without having adequate academic and professional degrees.

MOTIVATIONAL ORIENTATIONS AND BACKGROUND CHARACTERISTICS

The motivational orientations of our respondents behind their choice of occupation have also been examined in relation to variables, such as sex, rural-urban background and economic status, assuming that these may have influenced their orientations (Table 5.2). While examining these variables, the responses under the categories 'altruistic orientation', self-orientations etc., which were negligible, were clubbed as 'other factors'.

In the case of sex, we find that while male and female librarians did not differ in respect of 'chance entry' and 'other factors', it is interesting to note that female librarians tended to be only slightly less pragmatic as compared to their male counterparts. Because in India by and large women are not principal bread-winner.[27] In the prevailing conditions employed women is preferred in urban middle class families. Thus women are emerging as subsidiary bread-winner. This also explains why women librarians have slightly more academic orientation. It has also been found in a number of studies that women enter the job market not mainly for dire economic necessity but for supplementing the family income for maintaining higher standard of living.

TABLE 5.2: **Motivation for the Choice of Occupation by Background Characteristics (%)**

Background of Librarians	Type of Motivating Factors				Total
	Chance entry	Pragmatic	Academic or professional	Others	
Sex					
Male (N=135)	31.8	31.8	23.7	12.7	100.0
Female (N=65)	30.8	26.1	29.9	13.2	100.0
Rural & Urban Background					
Rural (N=49)	40.8	22.4	24.5	12.3	100.0
Urban (N=145)	29.7	31.7	25.5	13.1	100.0
Economic Status					
Well-off and average (N=55)	25.4	30.9	30.9	12.8	100.0
Low or difficult (N=128)	35.9	28.9	24.2	11.0	100.0

It may also be observed that more librarians from rural families had entered the profession by chance (40.8 per cent) as compared to the librarian of urban families (29.7 per cent). It seems that lack of adequate occupational information among rural librarians might have prompted their accidental entry into the profession. In respect of economic status, we also observe that chance factor has played some role in the choice of occupation in the case of librarians having low economic background.

CAREER MOBILITY

The pre-entry motivational orientations of a person are likely to change when he undergoes occupational socialisation and when he becomes involved in the organisational career. Thereafter, his career motivations are conditioned by the reward systems, and problems and contingencies associated with work-organisations. He may enter the organisation at the stage where good prospects for advancement stimulate him into working hard and striving for a better position. He may be dissatisfied with the working conditions of his organisation and consequently, he may like to play safe or look elsewhere for a better or different career. It has also been seen that if a professional person is not happy with his organisation role, he may likely to move to some another organisational even forgoing some economic gains. At times it may also be possible that lack of alternatives elsewhere may force him to develop loyalty to an organisation and commitment to his career.

Studies on career pattern of librarians reveal that there are two possible ways through which librarians may advance their career: (a) either by remaining within one system or organisation, or (b) by moving from one library to another. The former source of mobility is commonly referred as system of promotions and the latter may be considered as movement between organisations or inter-organisational mobility. As experience is supposed to be an essential factor in the advancement of career, data concerning only those respondents who had more than five years of experience in their professional career was taken in to consideration. Thus, the total respondents, we found that only 82 per cent were eligible for the above enquiry.

Our findings of the career mobility of the librarians (Table 5.3) reveal that one-third of them had immobile career. That is, they were stagnating at the same position where they first started their career. (Data regarding the career of immobile librarians have also been presented in Table 5.4). The remaining 66.5 per cent of librarians show upward mobility in their career. Examining the sources of mobility it may be noted that the system of promotion seems to be extremely biased in favour of male librarians. Recognizing that the nature and extent of mobility would differ from individual to individual it would be worthwhile to investigate the factors which might have influenced our respondents in their career mobility. In this respect, our analysis is confined to only some background variables, such as sex, rural-urban background, level of professional qualification, length of experience, and type of recruitment (Table 5.4).

Regarding sex, we find that the career mobility among male librarians is higher (73.1 per cent) as compared to females (51 per cent). In other words, nearly half of women librarians (49 per cent) had immobile career as against only one-fourth of male librarians. As the working women combine the dual roles of family and job they are less likely to be mobile if that would dislocate their family arrangements.

TABLE 5.3: **Career Mobility Among Librarians by Sex (%)**

Sources of Mobility	Male	Female	Total
None (N=55)	18.9	14.6	33.5
Inter-Organisational mobility (N=77)	34.2	12.8	47.0
Promotions (N=32)	17.0	2.5	19.5
Total (N=164)	70.1	29.9	100.0

TABLE 5.4: **Career Mobility by Background Characteristics (%)**

Background of Librarians	Mobility	Immobility	Total
Sex			
Male (N=115)	73.1	26.9	100.0
Female (N=49)	51.0	49.0	100.0
Rural Urban			
Rural (N=39)	100.0	0.0	100.0
Urban (N=121)	58.6	41.4	100.0
Professional Qualification			
Degree Holder (Minimum) (N=102)	63.7	36.3	100.0
M.Lib.Sc. Degree (Higher Level) (N=62)	71.0	29.0	100.0
Length of Experience			
6 to 10 years (N=48)	54.2	45.8	100.0
11 to 20 years (N=73)	71.2	28.8	100.0
21 and above (N=43)	72.0	28.0	100.0
Types of Recruitment			
First recruitment as para-professional (N=38)	94.7	5.3	100.0
First recruitment as professional (N=126)	57.9	42.1	100.0

Immobility among female librarians has always been focused in several studies which deal with the career patterns of librarians. Schiller[28] and Blankenship[29] in two independent studies examined job mobility of college and university librarians and both found that female librarians were less mobile than their male counterparts. Blankenship[30] had reported that 69 per cent of the females remained in the same jobs for 16 or more years, compared with 30 per cent of the males. Similarly, Harvey,[31] Morrison[32] and Carpenter and Shearer[33] found that women librarians were less mobile and men were more likely to change their positions.

Interestingly, all respondents from rural-backgrounds had mobile career as compared to their counterparts of urban-origins (58.6 per cent). Our data reveal that a sizable number of rural librarians (36 per cent) had started their career below the level of professional librarian so they had higher rate of movements between organisations in search of suitable jobs.

As indicated, the length of experience is an important factor for mobility. The highly and moderately experienced librarians show higher rate of mobility as compared to less experienced professionals. It may be that generally well-experienced professionals are recruited on middle and senior level positions in the libraries, and therefore they have greater chances of mobility as compared to their younger colleagues.

Further, we observed that librarians who had their initial appointments as para-professional, had higher rate of career mobility (94.7 per cent) as compared to their colleagues who joined the profession as trained librarians. Obviously, if initial placements would be on lower level of jobs, individuals are more likely to move upwards. In case of rural librarians, as stated above, we have seen that they were more mobile. But the point to be considered is that they were mobile not because of their rural environment but because of the fact they were not placed initially better in their career. In this respect, it needs to be noted that as the lower staff of the libraries are governed by the internal promotion policy of the organisation, such librarians who started their career as para-professionals would naturally experience more upward mobility in their career. On the other hand, we find that librarians, who were initially appointed on professional positions, were stagnated in their career because there are limited positions on senior and middle level in the profession, and even these are filled up by open selection. It is also to be noted that even the acquisition of high level of professional qualification (i.e., M. Lib Sc. degree) does not much brighten the chance of upward mobility.

EXTENT OF MOBILITY

The extent of mobility (Table 5.5) would mean in our context how many times a person has experienced upward mobility in his career either remaining in one organisation, or by moving from one organisation to another organisation. The extent of mobility has been described as 'one time' (i.e., one advancement in the career or one shift of job between organisations), 'two times' and 'three and more times'.

TABLE 5.5: **Extent of Career Mobility Among Librarians by Sex (%)**

Mobility	Male (N=115)	Female (N=49)	Total 164
None (N=55)	18.9	14.6	33.5
One time (N=58)	24.4	10.9	35.3
Two times (N=31)	15.9	3.1	19.0
Three and more times (N=20)	10.9	1.3	12.2
Total (N=164)	70.1	29.9	100.0

While examining the extent of mobility in relation to sex (Table 5.5), we find that female respondents differ sharply from males in respect of 'two and three movements'. It is clear that careers of an overwhelming majority of female librarians got stabilised after first movement, while only a small percentage of them had experienced two or three movements in their career. As hinted earlier, most of the female members assume job responsibilities only to support the income of their families, therefore, they would not like to move out independently of their spouses and households. This supportive tendency among them does not stimulate job aspirations in their career. Evidently men would strive more for advancement in their careers if opportunities are made available to them.

INTER-ORGANISATIONAL MOBILITY

Data regarding movements of librarians between organisations have also been examined. In order to study their inter-organisational mobility, the present placements of respondents have been viewed against their initial placements in different types of libraries (Table 5.6). It has already been mentioned earlier that libraries vary greatly not only in their aims and objectives but also in terms of their salary structure. It is rather common experience that good salary structure or prestige attached to the institution or both would act as motivating factors for career mobility. Therefore, an enquiry into this aspect would be fruitful.

TABLE 5.6: **Inter-Organisational Mobility Among Librarians (%)**

Present placement of Respondents	Initial placement of Respondents					
	School	College	University	Public	Special	Total
University Libraries (N=22)	13.6	36.4	18.2	13.6	18.2	100.0
Public Libraries (N=15)	46.6	33.3	6.7	6.7	6.7	100.0
Special Libraries (N=40)	12.5	17.5	10.0	2.5	57.5	100.0
Total (N=77)	19.5	25.9	11.7	6.5	36.4	100.0

It may be recalled that 77 respondents (47.0 per cent) had experienced inter-organisational mobility (Table 5.3). Data presented in Table 5.6 show the initial placements of these organisationally mobile librarians in relation to their present placements.

As regards mobility of librarians between different types of libraries, the general tendency is to move out from school and college libraries to other types of libraries. In university libraries, half of the population of librarians were migrants from schools (13.6 per cent) and colleges (36.4 per cent). Whereas in public libraries, the percentage of migrant librarians from the same sectors (i.e. from schools 46.6 per cent and colleges 33.3 per cent) was around eighty. But in the case of special libraries we find that only 42.5 per cent of librarians were migrants from other types of libraries, while majority of them had moved from the same type of libraries. It may also be noted that librarians who migrated from university libraries to the public and special libraries constitute only negligible proportions.

The following points may be highlighted in regard to career mobility of librarians:

(1) As the libraries of schools and colleges provide limited promotion possibility, professionals usually have moved out in search of better career in other types of libraries, after their initial placements.
(2) Besides the initial placements of professionals in any university or special libraries, the subsequent entry into these set of libraries is restricted to only those professionals who have enough experience in the same type of organisational set-up. In other words, the nature of organisation in which one starts ones career may act as a critical factor in his or her subsequent movements.
(3) The developments in science and technology have resulted in the establishment of large number of special libraries, which provide openings for experienced professionals. Professionals in the special libraries move only in one set of libraries.
(4) As university libraries provide uniform salary scales, the least inter-organisational movements have been experienced by professionals in these libraries.

Thus, we find that inter-organisational mobility is of two types: (a) the mobility of professionals from low-status, low paid organisations to high-paid and high-status organisations and (b) once placed in the second category of organisations, the tendency is to move in the same set of organisations because of specialisation and technical knowledge required.

CAREER IMMOBILITY

In view of the fact that one-third of respondents had not experienced any upward mobility in their careers, it is more preferable to examine the reason for career immobility. Immobile librarians who were in grip of stagnation, would ultimately be expected to resort 'organisational strategy' or 'stability strategy' for their careers, as discussed in Chapter One. Results from Slater's study[34] on career pattern and mobility of British librarians also indicate: "what the profession seems to be suffering from at the moment is immobility". In a study of college teachers of Delhi, it was noted that "a large majority (82.99 per cent) of academicians had begun their academic career as lecturers and were lecturers at the time of study without much hope for any change".[35] As compared to college teachers of Delhi, it would appear that librarians are definitely more upwardly mobile in their careers. But in reality this is not the case as there are multiplicity of career structures in the library profession. Contrary to the librarianship, the teaching profession has uniform career structure throughout the country in terms of pay-scales and positions (i.e., lecturership, readership and professorship). Additionally, the profession also prescribes the uniform entry point and the system of recruitment.

As against only three or four pay scales for teachers, there are at least 57 pay scales for trained librarians available in different organisations.[36] Even the Fourth Pay Commission of Government of India[37] found it difficult to rationalise the multiplicity of pay scales in the case of librarians and recommended a separate committee to look into this aspect. The Commission observed:

> There is no uniformity in the recruitment qualifications and posts with identical designations do not always have the same qualifications. , . . About 60 per cent posts of librarians are in the pay scales of Rs. 260-430, 330-560, 425-700, 550-900 and 650-1200. The remaining posts are spread over some 20 other scales. . . . There are difficulties in reclassifying the posts of librarians and specifying their qualifications and recruitment levels. The pay scales, qualifications and recruitment levels of responsibility will really depend on several factors, mainly on the size of the library, its character and importance. To draw up suitable proposals in this regard a committee may be constituted to undertake this work.[38]

Evidently, the higher rate of mobility, among the librarians of Delhi, as noticed against the college teachers of the same city, only indicates that they had random movements between organisations or sectors in search of slightly better remuneration, where 'they could get a frozen refuge'.

OCCUPATIONAL PRESTIGE

Some occupations are allocated greater prestige in the society on account of being functionally important. Studies on occupational prestige, invariably indicated that prestige hierarchies of occupations were found to be almost identical in most of the modern societies or groups.[39] Attempts have been made in several countries[40] including India[41] to grade the occupations according to some definite criteria.

Sociologically speaking prestige is not exactly the same thing as status or social position. Generally prestige may be said to represent the "subjective value granted to the perceived cluster of habits, objects and expectations associated with statuses of a given position".[42] However, the general public, usually do not make any distinction between prestige and status. For them, prestige happens to be an expression of socio-economic status of a given occupational category. An alternative method[43] suggested for the evaluation of occupational prestige is the self-evaluation of a professional group. In order to know the perception of prestige of librarianship as a profession in society, we asked three questions to the respondents. First of all, we asked them to mention two occupations which they would rate higher than librarianship. Similarly, respondents were asked to indicate two professions which they would consider equal to their own profession. Lastly, they were asked to identify any two professions which carry lower prestige than librarianship. It may be mentioned here that while all the respondents indicated names of professions which they considered to be higher and equal to librarianship, their assessments regarding the third question were confined to only 55 per cent of respondents. Therefore, respondents' perceptions concerning professions having lower status than librarianship have not been analysed. On the basis of the responses, it was possible to categorise the professions in terms of remaining two prestige-dimensions (Table 5.7).

In the first category, names of such professions which have been identified as more prestigious by respondents in comparison to librarianship have been presented. Among these professions, medicine has been identified as the most prestigious. The profession which comes next to the medicine, is teaching in universities and colleges. Traditionally the legal professions is regarded as highly prestigious but our respondents place lawyers and judges below scientists and engineers and officials of the superior administrative services, such as Indian Administrative Services, Indian Foreign Services, etc. Next to the lawyers, the personnel of defence and police services have been rated higher by ten per cent of respondents. The members of "other professions" which have been perceived higher than librarianship by negligible percentage of respondents are computer scientists/programmers, journalists and artists, bank employees and subordinate administrative staff.

TABLE 5.7*: **Respondents' Perceptions of Professions in Relation to Librarianship**

Category 1	*Category 2*
Professions having higher prestige than librarianship	Professions having equal prestige
Medical doctors (51.5)	School Teachers (59.0)
University and College Teachers (44.0)	Subordinate administrative services (31.5)
Scientists and Engineers (36.0)	College teachers (24.5)
Superior-administrative Services (28.0)	Journalists/artists (16.5)
Lawyers and Judges (11.5)	Nursing (12.5)
Defence and Police Services (10.0)	Programmers (10.5)
Others (19.0)	Others (35.5)

* Figures in parentheses indicates percentages. In each category, respondents were asked to identify two professions, hence the total percentage in each category comes to 200.

The occupations which were equally prestigious in relation to librarianship have been presented in the second category. There are seven professions in this category. It would be worthwhile to mention at the outset that majority of respondents (59.0 per cent) equate librarians with school teachers. Besides that, nearly one-third of respondents (31.5 per cent) are of the opinion that librarians are similar to the staff performing subordinate types of administrative jobs. As we have noticed that while majority of respondents consider librarians comparable to school teachers, there are at least one-fourth of respondents who want to place them equal to the college teachers. Since a section of university and college librarians enjoy the pay scales and other benefits equal to teachers, it is natural for them to consider their profession equal to college teaching.

In this context, it may be recalled that 44 per cent of respondents in the first category had considered university and college teachers being superior to librarians. As university or college teachers were rated higher and equal both by the respondents in relation to librarianship, it would be interesting to reveal their academic and professional background. Our data reveal that majority of respondents who considered librarianship inferior to college teaching, were found to be working on lower professional level having only minimum educational and professional qualifications. On the other hand, those respondents who were working on middle and senior levels with higher academic and professional qualification evaluated their profession equal to the college teachers. Besides this, a small percentage of professionals who were placed on lower professional level but having high academic and professional qualifications also rated librarianship as equal to the college teachers.

The other professional categories comparable to librarians are journalists (16.5 per cent), nurses (12.5 per cent) social workers (10.0 per cent) and programmers (10.5 per cent). It is also interesting to note that about one-third of respondents rate themselves equal to doctors (9.0 per cent), lawyers (4.5 per cent) and engineers (1.5 per cent) etc., as included in "others".

It is clear that most of the respondents consider librarianship as semi-professions such as school teaching, nursing, social work, etc. and they place it lower to full-fledged professions such as medicine, university teaching, engineers etc. Interestingly Slater[44] also made an attempt to investigate the prestige dimension of librarianship and found that twelve occupations were placed higher than librarianship by library and information science professionals of Great Britain. In that investigation some of the professional categories which were ranked higher than librarianship included doctors, scientists, solicitors, architects, lecturers, engineers etc.

Evidently, librarians' self-location of their profession places them in the category of semi-professions. In the process of professionalisation, many of the semi-professions including librarianship, would adopt different strategies to achieve the status of full-fledged professions. As income is functionally related to the prestige, members of many aspiring occupations, would likely to agitate for getting higher income in the society in order to improve their prestige. In order to bargain from the society, they would attempt to increase the knowledge base of their profession, institute higher level of training and formulate standards to raise the quality of their performance. Consequently, the process of recruitment would be strengthened and only motivated and qualified persons would be allowed entry to the profession.

OCCUPATIONAL SATISFACTION

An important aspect of occupational career is satisfaction which a professional derives from his career. We assumed that such an inquiry would be indicative of their occupational role commitment. Analysing the extent of satisfaction, we find that only 22 per cent of respondents reported that "it is the only career that could really satisfy me" and 42 per cent of them said that "it is one of the several careers which I could find almost equally satisfying". In contrast, 24 per cent of respondents expressed that librarianship was not "the most satisfying career that they could think of" and 12 per cent described their career as the "least satisfying". While combining the positive responses about job satisfaction, we find that majority of respondents (64 per cent) are satisfied with their career while more than one-third of them (36 per cent) are dissatisfied with their profession. Interestingly, Sergean[45] identified an identical percentage (i.e., 36 per cent) of dissatisfied library and information science professionals in Great Britain. In the case of another semi-professional category in India, i.e., of secondary school teachers, Ruhela's[46] findings revealed that the teachers turned out to be less professional and less satisfied with their career. From Oommen's study[47] we find that an overwhelming majority of doctors (85 per cent) were found to be highly satisfied with their careers.

It may be known that librarians and teachers differ from doctors in respect of social origins, motivational orientations and status of their occupations. In the case of doctors, their higher socio-economic background, their achievement ethos and the amount of prestige and money which they derive from the medical profession make them highly satisfied. On the other hand, the lower socio-economic background of librarians and teachers, their instrumental motive and the amount of deprivations which they experience from their occupation in terms of money and prestige do not provide "most satisfying career" for most of them.

FACTORS INFLUENCING CAREER SATISFACTION

Occupational satisfaction has also been examined in relation to some background variables. It is clear from Table 5.8 that sex is an important determinant of career satisfaction: 80 per cent of women librarians were satisfied with their career as compared to 56.3 per cent men. Again 26.3 per cent women were highly satisfied while only 20 per cent men expressed high degree of satisfaction.

The greater satisfaction among lady teachers was also reported by Ruhela in these words:

More women than men teachers expressed satisfaction with their salaries, and more men teachers than women teachers reported that they were not getting grades according to their qualifications. Most of the men teachers were worried about their financial problems, and so resorted to tuition work which they themselves admitted was unprofessional but essential for their survival.[48]

As men are the principal bread-winners, for their families, they aspire for more money in their jobs. Obviously very few male members in teaching and libraries achieve higher scales. Hence, there is a greater degree of dissatisfaction among them in this respect. On the other hand, women are usually not the principal bread-winners and in this respect their roles are only subsidiary in the family. They are non-careerist. So they do not suffer on account of less money and prestige as compared to their counterparts. Hence, there is a greater degree of satisfaction among the female professionals.

TABLE 5.8: **Career Satisfaction by Background Characteristics (%)**

Background of Librarians	Satisfied	Dissatisfied	Total
Sex			
Male (N=135)	56.3	43.7	100.0
Female (N=65)	80.0	20.0	100.0
Experience			
Up to 5 years (N=36)	77.7	22.3	100.0
6 to 10 years (N=48)	60.4	39.6	100.0
11 to 20 years (N=73)	69.9	30.1	100.0
21 years and above (N=43)	46.5	53.5	100.0
Types of Library			
University (N=83)	73.5	26.5	100.0
Public (N=33)	48.5	51.5	100.0
Special (N=84)	60.7	39.3	100.0
Type of recruitment			
Recruited as Para-professional (N=50)	82.0	18.0	100.0
Recruited as Professional (N=150)	58.6	41.4	100.0

The higher rate of satisfaction which female librarians derive in their career seems to be rooted in the nature of the library profession itself. Needless to mention that different occupations in the society carry different values and the females who join the profession usually do not have the same value orientations as possessed by their male counterparts. Women are more oriented towards working in an occupation which allows helping others. While men prefer occupations which can provide them money and status and allow freedom in their work place. Since librarianship lacks both these elements to a greater extent, it is quite natural that a section of male librarians would be dissatisfied from the profession. On the other hand, the women librarians who were drawn largely from good socio-economic backgrounds, do not suffer too much on account of money and prestige they get. Marie Mies[49] and Kala Rani[50] both have noted that the working women were quite satisfied with their job situations. They found them having little complaint both at the work-place and in the family because of their limited expectations. Since women combine both the roles successfully, they experience little conflict in their roles and therefore, seem to be greatly satisfied with their careers.

Our data show that the professionals seem to be highly satisfied in the initial years of their careers. During this period professionals usually have low expectations about promotion and they also have moderate mobility as they prefer to remain in one organisation in order to gain experience.

It may be seen that the professionals also experience moderate to higher degree of satisfaction in the second or third phase of their careers because majority of them achieve some advancements in their careers as a result of inter-organisational mobility or promotional policy. But when they reach senior levels, their dissatisfaction increases because of limited number of senior positions in the organisations. They have also self-imposed restrictions on mobility because they would lose many other benefits which they might have acquired as a result of their long service with the employing organisations. Thus, their level of satisfaction decreases in the last phase of their careers compared to the previous.

Our data reveal that the type of organisation in which professionals perform their roles is likely to influence their career satisfaction. The university and special libraries provide greater role satisfaction to the respondents. In our investigation, regarding the respondents' preference for organisational set-up, we discovered that majority of them (59.5 per cent) opted to work in special libraries because of specialised nature of client service in these organisations. Due to subject specialisation, the special librarians experience greater rate of mobility in their career seems to be the source of their job satisfaction. In the university library system since some professionals also enjoy pay-scales and other benefits equal to the academic staff, they also feel satisfied. But, the position of public librarians is entirely different. They are in the most disadvantageous positions on account of their generalised role performance, lower-scales of pay, and lack of upward mobility in their career. The result is that over half of the respondents (51.5 per cent) find their career in public libraries 'least satisfying'.

It may be recalled that we have categorised the respondents on the basis of their recruitment. We noticed, as mentioned earlier, that one fourth of our respondents joined the library as para-professionals who acquired on-the-job academic and professional qualifications, and achieved the status of professional librarians through the process of mobility. The rest two-thirds of them were directly recruited as professional librarians. We assumed that professionals in the former group with their pre-professional background or experience are likely to differ in their attitude or behaviour as compared to these in the latter.

When the career satisfaction of respondents was examined in relation to their type of recruitment, we find that 82 per cent of professionals with para-professional background are satisfied as compared with 58.6 per cent of professionals who were directly recruited to the profession. Analysing the degree of satisfaction, we notice that 36 per cent of respondents in the former group are highly satisfied as compared with only 18 per cent of respondents in the later group. It may further be emphasised that 41.4 per cent of directly recruited professionals are dissatisfied with their career. It may not be out of place to mention that among them nearly 15 per cent are highly dissatisfied with their career.

On the basis of the above finding, it may be said that if professionals experience upward mobility, they are likely to be satisfied with their occupational career. Therefore, what is important is not where they begin their career but how much they can move up. Hence, for the meaningful structuring of role activities of professionals it is necessary that employing organisations should create the necessary mobility-syndrome.

NOTES

1. Morris Rosenberg with the assistance of Edward A. Suchman and Rose K. Goldsen (1957), *Occupations and Values*, Glencoe, Illinois: Free Press.
2. Harry K. Schwarzweller (1960-61), "Values and Occupational Choice", *Social*

Forces, Vol. 39, pp. 126-35.

3. Richard L. Simpson and Ida Harper Simpson (1960-61), "Values, Personal Influence and Occupational Choice", *Social Forces*, Vol. 39, pp. 116-25.
4. S.R. Ranganathan (1940), *Preface to Library Science*, Delhi: University of Delhi, pp. 17-30.
5. Morris Rosenberg (1957), op. cit., pp. 3-4.
6. Peter M. Blau, John W. Gustad, Richard Jessor and Herbert S. Parnes (1956), "Occupational Choice: A Conceptual Framework", *Industrial and Labour Relations Review*, Vol. 9, pp. 266-79.
7. Carroll D. Clark and Noel P. Gist (1938), "Intelligence as a Factor in Occupational Choice", *American Sociological Review*, Vol. 3, pp. 638-94.
8. Edward K. Strong (1936), "Predictive Value of the Vocational Interest Test", *Journal of Educational Psychology*, Vol. 26, pp. 331-49.
9. Philip Elliot (1972), *The Sociology of Profession*, London: Macmillan.
10. Donald E. Super and R. Wright (1940), "From School of Work in the Depression Years", *School Review*, Vol. 49, pp. 120-30.
11. Lloyd G. Reynolds (1951), *The Structure of Labour Markets*, New York: Harper.
12. D.C. Miller and H.W. Form (1951), *Industrial Sociology*, New York: Harper, p. 651.
13. F.E. Katz and H.W. Martin (1962), "Career Choice Process", *Social Forces*, Vol. 41, pp. 149-54.
14. T.K. Oommen (1978), *Doctors and Nurses: A Study in Occupational Role Structures*, Delhi: Macmillan.
15. Ambika Chandani (1985), *The Medical Profession: A Sociological Exploration*, New Delhi: Jainsons.
16. *Ibid.*, p. 42.
17. T.K. Oommen (1978), op. cit., pp. 59-60.
18. Margaret Slater (1979), *Career Patterns and the Occupational Choice*, London: ASLIB (Occasional Publication, No. 23) p. 178.
19. R. Sergean (1977), *Librarianship and Information Work: Job Characteristics and Staffing Needs*, London: The British Library Research and Development.
20. Margaret Slater (1979), op. cit., p. 10.
21. Ralph H. Parker (1962), "Ports of Entry to Librarianship" in Philip H. Ennis and Howard W. Winger (eds.), *Seven Questions About the Profession of Librarianship* Chicago, Illionis: The University of Chicago Press, p. 51.
22. S.R. Ranganathan (1965-66), "Status of Library Personnel in India", *Library Herald*, Vol. 8, pp. 215-18.
23. *Ibid.*
24. G. Devarajan (1983), "Admission Seeking Variables in Library and Information Science Students: A Socio-economic Profile", *ALIS Bulletin*, Vol. 7, pp. 37-41.
25. T.K. Oommen (1978), op. cit., pp. 73-78.
26. *Ibid.*
27. The terms *Principal bread-winner* and *subsidiary bread-winner* have been suggested by Prof. T.K. Oommen in course of discussion for the analysis of the data.
28. Anita R. Schiller (1968), *Characteristics of Professional Personnel in College and University Librarians*, Urbana, Illionis: University of Illionis, Graduate School of library Science.
29. W.C. Blankenship (1967), "Head Librarians: How Many Men? How Many

Women?", *College and Research Libraries*, Vol. 28, pp. 41-48.

30. *Ibid.*
31. John F. Harvey (1957), *The Librarian's Career: A Study in Mobility* (ACRL Microcard Series No. 85), Rochester, New York: University of Rochester Press.
32. Perry D. Morrison (1969), *The Career of the Academic Librarian* (ACRL Monograph, No. 29), Chicago: American Library Association.
33. Raymond L. Carpenter and Kenneth D. Shearer (1972), "Sex and Salary Survey", *Library Journal*, Vol. 97, (November 15), pp. 3682-85.
34. Margaret Slater (1978), "Career Patterns and Mobility in the Library Information Field", *Aslib Proceedings* Vol. 30, pp. 344-51.
35. Arun P. Bali (1986), *College Teachers: Challenge and Responses*. New Delhi: Northern Book Centre.
36. A.K. Anand, Shabad Kapoor, and S.V. Malhan (1982), "Career Opportunities and Prospects for Library and Information Science Professionals in India, *ISASLIC Bulletin*, Vol. 27, pp. 72-92.
37. India, Central Fourth Pay Commission, Report, Part I, 1986, New Delhi, p. 205.
38. *Ibid.*
39. Robert W. Hodge (1966) et al., "Occupational Prestige in the United States: 1925-1963", in Reinhard Bendix and Seymour Martin Lipset (eds.), *Class, Status and Power*, pp. 322-34, 2nd edition, New York, The Free Press.
40. Robert W. Hodge (1966) et al., "A Comparative Study of Occupational Prestige", in Reinhard Bendix and Seymour Marlin Lipset, op. cit., pp. 309-21.
41. Victor D'Souza (1962), "Social Grading of occupations in India", *Sociological Review*, Vol. 1(2), New Series, July, pp. 145-59.
42. Theodore Caplow (1970), *The Sociology of Work*, Allahabad: Central Book Depot, (Published by arrangement with the University of Minnesota Press with the assistance of the Joint-Indian American Text Book Programme), p. 39.
43. G. Harries-Jenkins (1970), "Professionals in Organisations" in J.A. Jackson (ed.). *Professions and Professionalisation*. London: Cambridge University Press, p. 81.
44. Margaret Slater (1977), *Career Patterns and the Occupational Change*, London: Aslib (Occasional Publication, No. 23), p. 195.
45. R. Sergean (1977), *Librarianship and Information Work: Job Characteristics and Staffing Needs*, op. cit.
46. Satya Pal Ruhela (1984), "Professionalisation of School Teachers in India", Paper presented at the National Seminar on the Sociology of the Profession, (October 13-16, 1984); Department of Sociology, The University of Jodhpur (Mimeographed).
47. T.K. Oommen (1978), op. cit., p. 78.
48. S.P. Ruhela (1984), op. cit.
49. Maria Mies (1980), *Indian Women and Patriarchy: Conflicts and Dilemmas of Students and Working Women*, New Delhi: Concept.
50. Kala Rani (1976-77), "Performance of Job Role by Working Women", *Indian Journal of Social Work*, Vol. 37, and also see her *Role Conflict in Working Women*, New Delhi: Chetna Publications.

SIX

ROLE: COMMITMENT, PERCEPTION AND OBLIGATION

WHEN A person assumes an occupational label, he is legitimately expected to behave in an appropriate manner, though he may have different pre-entry motivations or level of professionalisation as compared with his peers. If he is an independent professional, his role expectations are determined predominantly by his professional organisation or peer group; in case he is an organisational professional, his role is likely to be moulded or shaped by his employing organisation or his own level of professionalisation. Role commitment, role perception and role obligation of library professionals — influenced or affected either by the internal structure of specific occupations or organisations or by the wider social structural elements — have been scrutinised here.

ROLE COMMITMENT

The term 'commitment' lacks consensus. Several researchers, such as Etzioni, Kanter, Staw and Salancik, developed different typologies to study organisational commitment.[1] Our conception of commitment is based on Becker's formulation as 'consistent line of activity'.[2] Role commitments have been examined from two dimensions: (a) Role commitment in regard to occupation as a whole and (b) Content of commitment. For investigation of the former respondents were asked about their willingness to continue in the occupation. When an individual enters an occupation he may have weak motivation in the beginning, but it is likely that he may develop strong role commitment when he realises ultimately that he has been 'locked up' in that occupation. His occupational training also binds him to remain in the same profession. His commitment may likely to be continued even if he is frustrated or alienated because the choice of career was his own. On the other hand if he is satisfied with his occupation he would like that his offsprings or kith and kin should also be in the same profession. undoubtedly, it would depend upon many factors such as his perceptions of prestige of his own occupation; achievements of his children or prevailing job situation.

The above aspect of commitment presents the instrumental perspective as one is committed to an occupation because he gets certain pay-off and amenities from it. But being a professional he is also 'committed' to internalisation of a body of knowledge, a self-imposed code of ethics, and work achievement. By all these he is rather obliged to increase his professional knowledge and to maintain relations with his professional organisations so that he may achieve excellence in professional role performance in relation to his clients.

DEGREE OF ROLE COMMITMENT: INSTRUMENTAL PERSPECTIVE

Role commitment of respondents in regard to first dimension was ascertained by a set of questions. The first one was, "Do you regret being in the profession?". It was assumed that those who expressed regret would not be fully committed to the profession. The degree of commitment in this case was recorded on a four-point scale: 'never', 'rarely', 'occasionally' and 'often'. It is significant to note that 42.5 per cent of respondents had no 'regrets' for joining the library profession. The respondents who 'rarely' regretted constitute 19.5 per cent. Thus, combining 'never' and 'rarely', 62.0 per cent of respondents appeared fully committed to the library profession. However, it is significant to note that as many as 38.0 per cent of respondents expressed their regret, those who 'often regretted' constitute 10.5 per cent and the remaining 27.5 per cent 'regretted' only ''occasionally'.

The second question asked to the respondents was: "Do you like to change to any other occupation?". It was expected that those professionals who were not committed or inadequately committed would like to change to other occupations. The data indicate that the majority of respondents (72 per cent) were not willing to change the profession; only 28 per cent of respondents had inclination to leave the profession taking up other jobs.

It is clear from the above analysis that majority of librarians are committed to their profession. In case of some other professionals like doctors, lawyers or military officers, it has been found that if they are committed to the profession, they would also like that their children to join the same profession. In order to ascertain whether the same tendency is prevalent among the librarians, we asked the following questions: (1) Would you advise your son to join your profession?, (2) Would you advise your daughter to join your profession?, (3) Would you advise others to join your profession?

It was observed that overwhelming majority of respondents would not advise their sons, daughters and others to join the profession of librarians. However, some would like to influence the careers of their sons (21 per cent), daughters (31 per cent) and other (32 per cent) in favour of librarianship. Thus, it is clear that notwithstanding the high role commitment of librarians they would not influence the occupational choice of their offsprings in favour of library profession. In this context, it was noted earlier that librarians place their profession in the category of semi-professions, such as school teaching, nursing, etc. Understandably, librarians hold high aspirations about their children and would like to see them in some prestigious professions. Similarly in the case of school teachers Ruhela[3] found that while they advise their daughters to be teachers, they do not want their sons to follow their footsteps. It is significant to note that a sizable section of librarians would prefer that their daughters to join the library profession. This shows that they consider librarianship as a favourable profession for females. Needless to say, this attitude partly contributes towards the feminisation of library profession.

PROFESSIONAL CONTENT OF COMMITMENT

Professional content of commitment or commitment to professional orientation was assessed through three items: (1) Membership of professional associations; (2) Attending professional meetings and (3) Reading professional journals. Responses to these items indicating above dimensions were consolidated to measure the content of commitment. The respondents' ratings on the scale of content of commitment were: 'high' 35.5 per cent, 'moderate' 32.0 per cent and 'low' 32.5 per cent. The findings are most disturbing. When respondents were measured on the first dimension of commitment (i.e., respondents' willingness to continue in the profession), it was found that the majority of them wished to continue in the profession. But surprisingly high professional content was reported only in the case of 35.5 per cent of respondents. As a member of a professional category, it is expected from them that they should be highly involved in professional activities and they should constantly make an attempt to increase their professional knowledge. But in the light of our data librarians' commitments to the profession can only be described as passive or instrumental. They do not seem to be highly attached to the professional activities and norms.

In order to ascertain whether the above trend is peculiar to librarianship or the same trend is also prevalent in respect of other professional groups such as teachers in the school and university system, a comparison is desirable. In the case of school teachers, Ruhela reports that "on the three variables, namely, Reading Index, attending Parent Teacher Association Meetings and attending meetings of professional associations, most of the teachers did not emerge as good professionals".[4] Surprisingly, university teachers also do not show high professional commitment, as revealed by Khanna[5] in her study. In the case of teachers of Jodhpur University it was reported by her that only 39.2 per cent of them had shown 'high' commitments towards the profession. In the light of the above findings, it can be argued that even teachers, whose role content is substantially academic are unable to manifest high professional commitment then it would be too much to expect from librarians a higher degree of professional commitment whose role content is substantially bureaucratic.

PROFESSIONAL CONTENT OF ROLE COMMITMENT BY BACKGROUND CHARACTERISTICS

Professional content of commitment has been examined in relation to respondents' background characteristics (see Table 6.1). Our data suggest that sex tends to influence the professional content of commitment to a greater extent. High commitment to profession was reported in the case of only 21.5 per cent of female librarians as against 42.2 per cent of male librarians. Females have always shown less commitment due to their dual roles. They feel "their primary responsibility towards their home so they become professional to a limited degree".[6]

Commitment to professional orientation also depends upon the amount of time one would spend on occupational training. Longer training period enforces higher commitment. Persons holding higher professional qualifications (Master's degree in Library and Information Science) show higher degree of commitments (48.7 per cent) than having only minimum professional qualifications (27.4 per cent).

It is evident from Table 6.1 that commitment to profession is also influenced by hierarchical positions of the respondents in the organisation. It may be noticed that one's commitment increases as one goes up in the hierarchy. Professional commitment among senior librarians is found to be higher (61.5 per cent) compared to the middle level (46.3 per cent) and junior librarians (19.1 per cent). It seems that senior professionals have more opportunities and time for professional development.

TABLE 6.1: **Professional Content of Commitment: Background Characteristics (%)**

Background Characteristics	Ranking of Respondents			Total
	High	Medium	Low	
Male (N=165)	42.2	31.1	26.7	100.0
Female (N=35)	21.6	33.8	44.6	100.0
Professional Qualifications				
Minimum (N=124)	27.4	36.3	36.3	100.0
Higher (N=76)	48.7	25.0	26.3	100.0
Rank				
Senior (N=124)	27.4	36.3	36.3	100.0
Middle (N=80)	46.3	30.0	23.7	100.0
Junior (N=94)	19.1	35.1	45.8	100.0
Career Mobility				
Upward Mobility (N=118)	43.2	32.2	24.6	100.0
No Mobility (N=82)	24.4	32.9	42.7	100.0
Types of Libraries				
University (N=83)	34.9	27.7	37.4	100.0
Public (N=33)	27.3	33.3	39.4	100.0
Special (N=84)	39.3	35.7	25.0	100.0

Upward mobility in one's career also increases the professional commitment. Role-occupants are greatly encouraged for professional activities if opportunities are made available to them for advancement in their careers. The data indicate that highly committed group of librarians (43.2 per cent) were those who were upwardly mobile. On the other hand lower commitments were seen in case of those librarians (24.4 per cent) who were stagnated in their careers.

The data regarding professional content of commitment have also been analysed in relation to the types of libraries. It was seen that the public librarians are less committed (27.3 per cent) to the profession as compared to their colleagues in special (39.3 per cent) and university (34.9 per cent) libraries. Evidently, it may be inferred that more professionalised nature of work organisations and clientele service in special and university libraries tend to increase the content of commitment among special and university librarians.

ROLE PERCEPTIONS

In order to understand the role perceptions of librarians we selected two hypothetical work situations and made an attempt to find out in what manner professionals would respond if faced with such situations. The two different work situations, though hypothetical in nature, reflect the real life situations which are often experienced by professionals working in the libraries. These situations represent some specific nature of role perceptions which have been explained further.

The first situation projected to them was: "Imagine a situation in which you have noticed that certain publications have not been properly classified or catalogued in your library". Since its implications are known to you, in what way will you react to it? There are two possible ways in which you might react to such a situation:

(i) I am not directly responsible for this, so I will ignore it.
(ii) I will personally discuss the matter with my colleagues in the processing section because I am confident that they would consider it as healthy criticism.

The two alternative responses indicate two distinct nature of role perceptions. It was considered that those respondents who would think "that the whole matter does not concern me or it is not under my purview" display bureaucratic orientation. But those librarians who would show much concern to the problem and would wish to remedy the same in the interest of their clients may be considered as having professional orientation.

It is encouraging to note (Table 6.2) that only a negligible percentage of respondents (9.5 per cent) perceived their role as bureaucratic, while overwhelming majority endorsed the professional orientation.

But the question arises whether the above situation may be considered as a prevalent one in the profession? We know that often there is a difference between what one thinks one would do and one's colleagues would. The perception of latter may give an idea as to what is the general situation in the profession. Therefore, we asked the respondents to indicate (in the same projected situation, as mentioned above): "In what way do you think most of your colleagues would like to react to it"?

TABLE 6.2: **Role Perception in Hypothetical Work Situation (%)**

		(Situation - 1)	
Nature of Role Perceptions	Self-role perception	Perceptions of colleagues' role	Extent of discrepancy
Bureaucratic	9.5	36.0	+ 26.5
Professional	90.5	64.0	– 26.5
Total	100.0	100.0	

Our underlying assumptions for assessing the respondents' perception about their colleagues' role seem to be valid when we observe the findings provided in Table 6.2. It is clear that there is substantial difference between 'self-perception of roles' and 'perception of roles of colleagues' in a given situation. It is found that respondents who perceive their role as bureaucratic constitute a tiny minority, whereas the same respondents perceive that at least 36 per cent of their colleagues would show bureaucratic attitude in dealing with the matter. The difference between perceptions of 'role for self' and 'role for colleagues' is also evident in the case of professional role orientation.

The above findings may lead to suggest that if a sizable percentage of librarians would hold bureaucratic role perceptions, they may likely to contribute to more bureaucratisation in library organisations.

The investigation regarding role perception of respondents has been further pursued by presenting another hypothetical situation for response. In this case attempts have been made to reflect the needs of the clients more clearly, so that respondents' real involvement for meeting clients needs could be assessed directly. The situation projected to them was: "Suppose, you are working in some public library. You have been assigned duty on reference desk. An unknown reader comes to you for getting some information just at the end of your office hours. There are several alternative responses to the situation:

(i) without giving much importance to his query, I will ask him to come next day;
(ii) I would like to solve his problems immediately, because it may provide me an opportunity to learn something new;
(iii) I would not mind to stay beyond my working hours because clientele service is my motto".

Like earlier situation, respondents were asked to select any one of the alternatives which they would like to opt for themselves. They were also asked to indicate how their colleagues are likely to deal with the same situation.

The three possible alternatives, as mentioned in the above situation, indicate three types of role orientation. It is expected that professionals who are bureaucratically oriented would resort to the first alternative which suggests that the user should visit next day in order to get answer for his queries. On the contrary, professionally-oriented respondents would like to solve their problems immediately because that would provide them opportunity to increase their knowledge. Similarly, those respondents who are service-oriented would also prefer to stay back so as to satisfy their client.

It is obvious from Table 6.3 that except for the few respondents (4.5 per cent) who tend to be bureaucratic, overwhelming majority of them are almost equally distributed on professional and client orientations in 'self-perception of their roles'. But when we take cognizance of their perceptions regarding their colleagues' role in the same situation, the extent of discrepancy is substantial. Regarding bureaucratic orientation, which represents negative aspect of the role perception in the present context, the gap is the greatest. In other words, nearly half of the respondents (44.5 per cent) perceive that their colleagues would behave in bureaucratic manner with their clients. Next to the bureaucratic orientation, our finding regarding client orientation is also disturbing. While 46 per cent of respondents perceive their 'self-role' to be client–oriented, surprisingly only half of them (23.0 per cent) would attribute the same role for their colleagues. However, in the case of professional orientation, there is less discrepancy between 'self-perception of roles' and 'perception of others'.

It may be noted that the role orientations such as professional and client have been treated separately because there is a difference in motivation between these two regarding the service to the clients. The professional who helps the clients with a motive to improve his or her knowledge, does not have service orientation as his or her primary consideration. But ultimately both these orientations are functional to situation as these provide service to the clients. The dysfunctional aspect of role content has been characterised by only bureaucratic orientation. Our data indicate that nearly half of the respondents view their colleagues' role as dysfunctional. The question arises as to why there is so much discrepancy regarding bureaucratic dimension of role orientation between self and others. Is it due to lack of cordiality in colleaguial relations or is it rooted in value orientations? The problem needs further investigation.

TABLE 6.3: **Role Perception in Hypothetical Work Situation (%)**

		(Situation - 2)	
Nature of Role Perceptions	Self-role perception	Perceptions of colleagues' role	Extent of discrepancy
Bureaucratic	4.5	44.5	+ 40.0
Professional	49.5	32.5	– 17.0
Client Orientation	46.0	23.0	– 23.0
Total	100.0	100.0	

ROLE OBLIGATIONS

Role obligation is another dimension which we intend to explore in this section. For this purpose, we asked the respondents: "While working in the library, to whom do you think you are discharging your duties? Respondents were asked to select any one of the following statements:

(i) I work for the users because, I get personal satisfaction;
(ii) I work for the maintenance of existing services in the library as part of my duty;
(iii) I work for encouraging the readership in the community.

It is significant to note that a majority of respondents (60.0 per cent) are of the view that they work for the users of the library. These categories of professionals derive satisfaction by serving their clients. In contrast, a sizable percentage (27.0 per cent) of professionals perceive their roles in terms of organisational responsibilities. They consider their role as part of their official duties. Interestingly, relatively few professionals (13.0 per cent) relate their services to the community or society at large.

These three types of role obligations have certain implications. The respondents who serve their clients with sole motive of deriving personal satisfaction from them may be labelled as inner-directed or person-directed. These professionals consider their users as a source of ego-satisfaction. Similarly those who think that they are serving the clients or maintaining different services in the libraries because they are employed or paid for that, may be designated as organisation-directed. These categories of professionals are more or less duty-bound. They prefer not to be emotionally involved with the clients. They interact with them in the framework of organisational rules and regulations. Finally, these professionals who consider their role-playing in the wider context of the society or community may be categorised as collectivity-directed. For the collectivity-directed professionals, users are part of a larger society and they do not owe any personal obligation to them. They perform unattached service to them.

Though all the role obligations are positive from the point of view of the clients, it is important to note that very few librarians have been able to place their roles in the context of the wider society. Their perceptions, however, seem to be fully insulated from the needs of their immediate clients or organisations. With their limited world view it seems that Indian librarians would be slow in contributing to the making up of an information society.

NOTES

1. See Richard M. Mowday, Lyman W. Porter and Richard M. Steers (1982), *Employee-Organisation Linkages: The Psychology of Commitment, Absentism and Turnover*. New York, Academic Press, pp. 20-26.
2. Howard S. Becker (1960), "Notes on the Concept of Commitment" *American Journal of Sociology*, Vol. 60, pp. 32-42.
3. Satya Pal Ruhela (1984), "Professionalisation of School Teachers in India", National Seminar of the Sociology of the Professions (October 13-16, 1984), Department of Sociology, University of Jodhpur (Mimeographed).
4. *Ibid.*
5. Kirti Khanna (1987), *Role Structure of Academics: A Profile of Jodhpur University Teachers*, Jodhpur, Jain Brothers, p. 113.
6. J. Bernard (1964), *Academic Women*, Pennsylvania, The Pennsylvania State University Press, p. 48.

SEVEN

ROLE IMAGES AND VALUE ORIENTATIONS OF LIBRARIANS

ROLE EXPECTATION is another important aspect in the theory of role analysis (Chapter One). The study of role expectations may be made through different aspects, viz., expectations held by role incumbents, expectations held by significant others (e.g., clients, colleagues, peers, etc.), and expectations held by outsiders. If we investigate the role incumbents' own definition of their roles, we may unfold their ideal role images. In this chapter, role images of librarians have been investigated in two contexts: their self-role images and their organisational role images.

SELF-ROLE IMAGES

Respondents were asked to indicate three qualities of librarians, in order of preference, for which they should be valued. The list of attributes provided to them may be grouped into three conceptual categories: client orientation, professional orientation and bureaucratic orientation. It may be made clear at the outset that these categories have been treated separately only for analytical purpose, though in reality, it would be extremely difficult to differentiate them. For investigating *client orientation,* we included items such as "willingness to give more time to users if he or she needs it", "helpful attitudes to the users", "ready to eliminate procedures for the benefit of users", and "ability to understand and identify with users," etc. *Professional orientation* is indicated by such items, as "willingness and ability to apply knowledge", "attending professional meetings", "willingness to innovate", "ability to do research", etc. Responses to the items such as "obedience to the superiors," "ability to maintain up to date records of the section or library", "following library rules strictly", etc. are taken as indicative of *bureaucratic orientation.*

Our data suggest (Table 7.1) that there is high content of client orientation in self-role image of ıibrarians. The majority of respondents indicate client orientation. Being professionals, it was expected from the librarians that they would score high on professional orientation. But on the contrary, we find that they scored low (18.5 per cent) on it. They are almost equally distributed on bureaucratic (16.0 per cent) and professional orientations (18.5 per cent).

TABLE 7.1: **Role Images of Librarians : Self and Organisational (%)**

Nature of Role images	Self image	Organisational image	Extent of discrepancy
Client Orientation	65.5	38.0	– 27.5
Professional Orientation	18.5	29.0	+ 10.5
Bureaucratic Orientation	16.0	33.0	+ 17.0
Total	100.00	100.00	

ORGANISATIONAL ROLE IMAGES

Respondents' self-evaluation of their roles have been described above. In the second context, we investigated the respondents' estimate of the organisational role images. For this purpose, we asked the respondents to identify three qualities of professional librarians (as mentioned in the case of ideal role images, in order of preference), which were actually valued in their organisations.

Organisational role images of respondents have been indicated in Table 7.1. Data regarding client orientation is quite disturbing. It may be noted that only 38 per cent of respondents felt that client orientation is actually valued in the organisations, while one-third of them define their roles in terms of bureaucratic elements. It is also clear that less than one-third of librarians do not estimate their roles in terms of professional orientation.

It is significant to note that while a majority of respondents project client orientation as their self-role image, they also think that there is a sharp decline in that role orientation as far as the organisations are concerned. In other words, we find that there is a greater discrepancy between self-role images and organisational role images. On the other hand, when we compare the bureaucratic orientations, we observe that it seems to be lower (16.0 per cent) in the self-role image but tends to become higher (i.e. more than double) (38.0 per cent) in the organisational contexts.

The above analysis raises an important question as to why there is a sharp decrease in the client orientation and a substantial increase in bureaucratic orientation in the context of two role images. Does it mean that high client orientation which respondents estimate ideally are likely to be thwarted by organisationally prescribed rules and regulations? Is it so that organisational patterns of libraries are not conducive to the advancement of service ideals of respondents? Does bureaucratic norms of the organisation come in conflict with the service ideals? Our doubts in this respect get strengthened when we find that bureaucratic orientation does not only get stabilised but rather reinforced in the organisational contexts. Therefore, logically it may be accepted that adherence to the established rules and procedures in the organisations may generally tend to affect the service-orientation of professionals.

Surprisingly, professional orientation which seems to be lower (18.5 per cent) in the self-role image of librarians tends to increase significantly (29.0 per cent) in the organisational contexts. It means that those respondents who use to undermine the value of professional role in their self-image now seem to develop the same in their work milieu. In other words, we find that discrepancy is positive in relation to professional orientations.

The extent of discrepancy between self-role image and organisational role image indicates that professionals are likely to experience role conflicts or role strains. If bureaucratic orientation tends to increase it might affect the service ethos or professional ethos of librarians. It has been generally seen that professionals tend to become bureaucratic if tasks in the organisation are not clearly demarcated into bureaucratic and professional aspects. Besides that, there are other factors too which may also contribute to the bureaucratic orientations such as low occupational prestige and low level of professionalisation. In the case of librarians, the high client orientation, as shown by them in their self-role images may be due to their low level of professionalisation. It has been found that usually those professions, which are not accorded high prestige place more emphasis on service-orientation in order to justify their existence or survival in the society. On the other hand, full-fledged professions, which enjoy higher prestige in social structure usually place high emphasis on professional orientations.

It may be expected that those librarians, who would give importance to professional roles in their work milieu, are likely to experience more role conflicts if their expectations are not met by their employing organisations. By implication, if organisations do not structure the roles of their professionals on models prescribed by the professions, it is likely that professionals may be alienated from their roles and as a result of that they may tend to ignore the welfare of the clients on the pretext of adhering to the bureaucratic norms.

FACTORS INFLUENCING SELF-ROLE IMAGES

The self-role images of both male and female librarians differ in respect of client and professional orientations (Table 7.2). The data suggest that the female librarians show high client orientation (72.3 per cent). At the same time they score low in professional orientation (12.3 per cent) as compared to the male librarians. Obviously female librarians undermine professionalism and attach more value to the client orientation. The low content of role commitment in the case of female librarians may be the consequence of their self-role image.

While a large number of professionals in all the ranks project client orientation as their dominant role, senior librarians seem to be less client-oriented (57.7 per cent) than middle level (67.5 per cent) and junior librarians (66.0 per cent). Besides client orientation, senior librarians (34.6 per cent) attach more value to professional roles than their subordinates, both junior (14.9 per cent) and middle level (17.5 per cent). They are also quite low (7.7 per cent) in respect of bureaucratic role images as compared to their middle level (15.0 per cent) and junior colleagues (19.1 per cent).

Our data suggest that professionalism is significantly related with higher hierarchical status. It may be safe to conclude that higher the rank of the role-occupants, greater their self-image of professional roles. In other words, the organisational status (which one usually expects to achieve in this profession after having enough professional experience and a great deal of mobility) seems to mould the role images of the professionals. Being new entrants to the profession, the junior librarians seem to be more concerned with rules and regulations of the organisation. In the initial phase of their career, the foremost task for them is to make themselves adaptable to the bureaucratic norms. Their role-activities include mostly routine — operations which have minimal professional - contents. Because of routine nature of their role-performance, they lack sufficient professional orientations in their role images.

When junior professionals move to the middle ranks, they are required to share many obligations of the organisation including the supervision of subordinate staff who usually perform routine-operations and "dirty jobs". In order to deal uniformly with their subordinates they usually try to stick to the set procedures. Thus, preoccupied with routine administrative duties, they do not find enough opportunity for their professional growth. Hence, it is quite likely that they do not place more value to professional orientation in their role images.

TABLE 7.2: **Self-Role — Images of Librarians by Background Characteristics (%)**

Background of Librarians	Nature of role images			Total
	Service orientation	Professional orientation	Bureaucratic orientation	
Sex				
Male (N=135)	62.2	21.5	16.3	100.0
Female (N=65)	72.3	12.3	15.4	100.0
Rank				
Senior Level (N=26)	57.7	34.6	7.7	100.0
Middle Level (N=80)	67.5	17.5	15.0	100.0
Junior Level (N=94)	66.0	14.9	19.1	100.0
Types of Libraries				
University (N=83)	72.2	14.5	13.3	100.0
Public (N=33)	54.6	12.1	33.3	100.0
Special (N=84)	63.1	25.0	11.9	100.0

However, the case of senior professionals is quite different. Being senior, they are placed with greater autonomy in the organisation. They are not involved into the routine activities of the libraries and are mainly concerned with the policy decisions. They are well assured that their experienced subordinates would take care of the proper maintenance of the client services. Endowed with autonomy they have enough opportunities for professional growth. In fact they are "cosmopolitans". They normally maintain close links with fellow professionals inside or outside the country. They are the persons who evaluate or sponsor the peers and juniors for suitable senior positions in the profession. They generally hold positions in professional associations or organisations. It is natural then, that they would place greater emphasis on professional orientation. Thus, it gives us some clue to suggest that higher content of professionalism tends to lower down the bureaucratic orientation and higher professionalism is anchored in existential higher status in the organisation.

The role images of respondents have also been viewed in respect of their work-settings. The findings suggest that organisational structures of the libraries tend to shape the role images of the librarians. It may be seen that client orientation is more higher among university (72.2 per cent) and special (63.1 per cent) librarians as compared to the public librarians (54.6 per cent). It is surprising that public librarians show lower client orientation in their role images. On the contrary, one could expect that public librarians should have projected more client orientation as they have major role to play in encouraging the reading habit among the masses. But it seems that the organisational structure of public libraries is not conducive for creating appropriate client orientation among public librarians. As a result they attach more value to bureaucratic norms as compared to their colleagues in university and public libraries.

The content of professional orientation is higher in the case of special librarians (25.0 per cent) compared to their colleagues in university (14.5 per cent) and public (12.1 per cent) libraries. Perhaps it may be so due to the influence of 'role others' who usually expect more professionalised service from the special librarians.

VALUE ORIENTATIONS IN ROLE IMAGES

It has been seen that a majority of librarians characterise their role images in terms of client orientation. It has also been noticed that high service ideals which they hold in their self-role image is not endorsed by their work organisations. The question arises as to what could be the possible reasons for erosion of such service ideals in addition to organisational constraints. If it is assumed that a particular value orientation is responsible in this regard it becomes necessary to find out whether librarians' role images are in conformity with their value orientations. In order to understand this, we wish to examine the following dimensions:

(1) What values do the librarians uphold in serving their clients; and
(2) What perspective they have in regard to clients service.

The value orientations of librarians have been explored with the help of three statements. The responses were recorded on a five point scale: 'strongly agree', 'agree', 'cannot say', 'disagree' and 'strongly disagree'. In the final analysis, we combined the first two categories of responses into one and treated it as 'positive'. Similarly, the last categories of responses were clubbed together and were considered as 'negative'. Responses on middle category, i.e., 'cannot say' were treated as neutral. The following are the statements administered to the respondents for unfolding their value orientations:

(1) "Whether the reader is satisfied with me or not, it does not bother me, so long as I deal with him according to the rules and regulations."
(2) "The professionals in the library should realise that helping the users directly would provide them an opportunity to grow professionally. Therefore, they should help the users and try to finish their specific work some way or the other."
(3) All professionals in the library should directly help the users even if they are placed in different sections or they have been assigned specific work.

The first statement puts emphasis on the strict observance of the rules and regulations of the libraries rather than working for the full satisfaction of the clients. The librarians who would agree to the statement have bureaucratic value orientation. The second statement presents professional perspective of client service. It suggests that the respondents would be benefited professionally by serving the clients. The third statement gives excessive importance to the client service. The librarians who would subscribe to such view may even be expected to go beyond their role-jurisdiction to serve the clients. Naturally such respondents would be labelled as client oriented.

It is obvious from Table 7.3 that only 16 per cent of respondents hold bureaucratic value orientations. It is extremely interesting to note that the same percentage of respondents indicated their bureaucratic perceptions in case of their self role images (see Table 7.1). We also find that 55 per cent of respondents show negative responses in regard to the bureaucratic values. It means that they hold positive values so far as client service is concerned. In this respect also the greater conformity between value orientations and self-role images of respondents may be recognised. It may be recalled that 65.5 per cent of respondents stated to be client-oriented in their self-role images (Table 7.1). It is also significant to note that less than one-third of respondents show ambivalent attitude in this regard. Therefore, it may be safe to think that those respondents, who hold neutral views regarding bureaucratic value orientations, are more likely to be moulded by the organisational norms. However, it is important to note that an overwhelming majority of respondents have professional and client oriented values.

TABLE 7.3: **Value-Orientations of Librarians (%)**

Value-Orientations	Direction of Value Orientations		
	Positive	Negative	Neutral
Bureaucratic	16.0	55.0	29.0
Professional	81.5	11.5	7.0
Client	76.5	16.5	7.0

PERSPECTIVES OF CLIENT SERVICE

Our investigation in the area of value orientations of librarians reveal that they hold very high positive values towards the service ideals. Therefore, it would be interesting to examine specifically what perspectives they have in regard to client-service. In order to elicit their opinion in this regard we administered the following three value statements and asked them to select one which they prefer most:

1. "Information plays a vital role in the development of a country, therefore demands of users should be immediately taken care of by the professionals."
2. "In case, the demands of the users are not met immediately, they will make complaints against the service to the library authorities therefore they should be attended to."
3. "Even when the demands of users cannot be met immediately or properly, they should be handled in such a manner that they should not fell neglected."

The three statements represent three different perspectives of client service. The first statement implies that users are not important by themselves, instead their information needs are important, because information is necessary input for development of a country. It denotes developmental perspective of client service. The second statement indicates that professionals are bound to serve the users because they are employed by the organisations for that purpose. Undoubtedly it brings in bureaucratic compulsion for providing client service. But the third statement is very different from the other two. It advises professional librarians to treat the users sympathetically even if the materials required by them are not available in the library. It presents humanitarian perspective in dealing with the clients.

Our data suggest that while more than half of the respondents (53.5 per cent) indicate developmental perspective in client service, a sizable number of them (40.5 per cent) also serve their clients with humanitarian motives. But respondents who hold bureaucratic perspectives of client service constitute only negligible percentage (6.0 per cent). Hence, it is clear that professionals are less likely to perform their roles under threat or compulsion from the organisation.

In sum, self-role image of librarians did not correspond with what they thought was their organisational role image. While the content of client orientation was higher in their definition of self-role image, the content of bureaucratic orientation was lower. In contrast, there was sharp decrease in the content of client orientation and substantial increase in the content of bureaucratic orientation in their definition of organisational role image. Thus, it may be suggested that organisational patterns of libraries do not seem conducive to the advancement of client orientation even though the librarians hold very high positive values towards it.

EIGHT

ROLE RELATIONS

ANY FORMAL organisation cannot be studied only on the basis of its structural characteristics. The individual characteristics of the role occupants and their perceptions of various factors in the settings or environment in which they perform their roles must be taken into consideration. The role of any category of employee in an organisational set-up cannot be understood without 'role-others'. In the role-set of librarians, we may envisage three basic types of role-relations — superior-subordinate relations; colleaguial relations and professional-client relations. In this part, we propose to discuss these aspects of role-relations.

SUPERIOR-SUBORDINATE RELATIONS

In any bureaucratic organisation, specialisation or ability is accommodated within a hierarchical framework. In other words, positions are ranked according to the degree of specialisation. Higher status in the organisation usually denotes greater specialisation. The status system in any organisation, thus corresponds closely to the hierarchy of superior-subordinate roles.

The superior-subordinate role is structured according to the rights and duties. The superior has the right to command, to allocate tasks, to delegate authority and to provide suitable rewards. On the other hand, the subordinate's role is characterised by obedience or loyalty. The superiors is supposed to possess abilities for guiding the subordinates and the latter should take guidance from the former. Besides striving for organisational goals, the superior should also be equally interested in the promotion of personal goals of subordinates (needs, satisfaction and motivation) within the institutional framework.

Bureaucratic Role Relatiions

Superior-subordinate relationship has been studied from two dimensions: bureaucratic and professional. In order to unfold bureaucratic role relations, we examined the perceptions of respondents regarding the delegation of authority by the superiors to the subordinates and the sharing of the organisational responsibilities by both the parties.

Delegation of Authority

Delegation of authority to the subordinates is generally accepted as one of the most desirable means of training the juniors in any organisation. Such delegation brings confidence in the subordinates and stimulates their growth potential. Delegation also expedites disposal of work. The need for adequate delegation down the hierarchy is even greater in service organisations so that delays in decision-making could be minimised.

Delegation of authority by superiors in organisations was assessed through the following statements:

(i) They delegate a *great deal* of authority;
(ii) They delegate *enough* authority to their subordinates;
(iii) They delegate *some but not enough* authority to their subordinates;
(iv) They delegate *very little* authority to their subordinates; and
(v) They *do not* delegate any authority to their subordinates.

Delegation of authority has been examined in case of only middle level and junior level professionals. The number of professionals in these categories are 174. The results show that nearly one-fourth of respondents perceive 'very little' (14.4 per cent) or 'no' delegation (9.7 per cent) of authority in their organisation. Respondents who perceive 'a great deal' of delegation authority constitute only 14.4 per cent. Nearly one-third of the respondents (32.2 per cent) perceive 'enough' delegation of power from their superiors, while 29.3 per cent of them feel that delegation is up to 'some' extent only. In other words, more than half of the respondents (61.5 per cent) perceive moderate delegation of power from their superiors. Perception of less delegation of power is higher (29.7 per cent) in the case of junior level professions as compared to the seniors (17.5 per cent). Understandably, the extent of delegation of power is dependent upon the readiness of subordinates to assume responsibility as well as the willingness of superiors to share responsibility. Therefore, it is necessary to investigate the perceptions of both superiors and subordinates in respect of assuming responsibility.

Superiors' Willingness to Share Responsibility

Perceptions of respondents regarding the superiors' willingness to share the responsibility in the organisation were assessed with the help of the following statements:

(i) They like to take *a great deal* of responsibility;
(ii) They like to take little more than *enough* responsibility;
(iii) They like to take *just enough* responsibility;
(iv) They like to take *very little* responsibility; and
(v) They *do not* like to take any responsibility.

Respondents who were selected for this aspect of investigation belonged to middle and junior levels. They were asked to select one of the above statements which they would think to be the most appropriate in their case.

One-fourth of respondents (27.6 per cent) feel that their superiors themselves retain a great deal of responsibility. That is, they rarely share the responsibility with the juniors. Less than one-fourth of them (22.4 per cent) think that they take 'very little' (17.8 per cent) or 'no' responsibility (4.6 per cent) in organisational matters. In other words, they pass their responsibilities either to their immediate juniors or to their immediate seniors in the hierarchy. The remaining half of the respondents (fifty per cent) are of the view that their seniors assume 'enough' or 'more than enough' responsibility of their work.

The respondents of the study clearly indicate that the senior librarians are greatly involved in the management of the libraries through a process of sharing responsibilities. It is expected that seniors' willingness to share responsibility with their juniors would likely to increase the level of participation of the juniors in regard to organisational matters. The foregoing results show that their subordinates perceive that senior librarians are highly committed to the performance of their roles.

Subordinates' Willingness to Assume Responsibility

As indicated, the delegation of power in an organisation will depend not only upon the willingness of superiors in sharing responsibility but also the readiness of juniors in assuming responsibility. Therefore, we analysed the opinions of both seniors and middle level librarians regarding their subordinates in respect of assuming responsibility. The following statements were used to assess the perceptions of seniors regarding their subordinates' willingness to assume responsibility:

(i) They are not willing to take *any* responsibility;
(ii) They are willing to take *very little* responsibility;
(iii) They are willing to take *some but not enough* responsibility;
(iv) They are willing to take *enough* responsibility;
(v) They are willing to take a *great deal* of responsibility.

Respondents were asked to select any one of the above statements which they would think to be the closest to their feelings.

While one-fourth of the seniors (25.5 per cent) perceive that their subordinates are willing to assume 'a great deal' and 'enough' responsibility, it is also interesting to note that almost the same percentage of them (27.3 per cent) think that they are not willing to take any responsibility or they take 'very little' responsibility. However, nearly half of the superiors (47.2 per cent) are of the opinion that their juniors are willing to take 'some' type of responsibility.

Whereas almost one-fourth of seniors (27.6 per cent) do not like to share any kind of responsibility with their juniors, one-fourth of subordinates also are unwilling to assume responsibility. Based on the perceptions of both superiors and subordinates, it may be said that one-fourth of professionals in each of these categories wish to remain non-committal or unwilling to share or assume any responsibility. Therefore, it cannot be hoped that all professional members would participate equally to achieve the goals of organisations.

Elements of Professional Orientation in Superior-Subordinate Relations

The professional orientation in role relations has been assessed through a set of two questions:

(i) Do your superiors suggest to you to read or write something of professional interest?
(ii) Do you suggest to your subordinates to read or write some-

thing of professional interest?

The first question was administered to 94 junior professionals and the second question was addressed to 174 senior and middle level professionals. The responses were recorded separately on a four point scale: 'never', ''rarely', 'frequently' and 'most often'. Our assumptions were that those superiors who would be interested in the professional growth of their subordinates would like to suggest to their juniors 'reading or writing something of professional interest: 'frequently' and/or 'most often'. Such type of superiors may be labelled as 'Professional-equalitarian'. On the other hand, there may be another type of superiors who would like to confine themselves only to the routine activities of the organisations and are not interested in the professional growth of their subordinates. Such type of superiors may be categorised as 'bureaucratic-authoritarian'.

Based on the perceptions of juniors, nearly sixty per cent (59.0 per cent) of superiors were labelled as 'bureaucratic-authoritarian'. It means that such superiors do not have concern for the professional development of the juniors. Superiors who were of professional-equalitarian type also constitute a sizable group (41.0 per cent). Therefore it may be inferred that a higher degree of professionalism would not be fostered if superior-subordinate relationships are mainly of bureaucratic-authoritarian type.

As indicated, attempts were also made to know the types of orientations superiors hold about their juniors. Contrary to the perceptions of juniors, majority of superiors (69.0 per cent) perceived themselves as professional-equalitarian while less than one-third of them (31.0 per cent) described themselves as bureaucratic professional. The discrepancy existing between these two types of perceptions is not surprising as the similar discrepancy was observed in the case of 'self-perception of roles' and 'perception of roles by others'.

COLLEAGUIAL RELATIONSHIP

Colleaguial relationship is one of the essential aspects of professionalism. According to Ranganathan,[1] achievement in the field of library science, which comprises the technique, the knowledge, the role and purpose of profession would depend inescapably on the quality and strength of trained personnel, i.e., profession of librarians. Therefore, professional goal should be achieved *together* and with a *devotion*. For guiding the professional fraternity in this regard, Ranganathan wished that one should keep in mind the following ideals suggested by the Rigvedic seers:

> Meet together, talk together, understand aright.
> Pray in common, achieve in common let there be unity and understanding.
> Alike be your intentions, harmonious your feelings.
> And concerted your thoughts, so there may be complete union among you.[2]

The present study also makes an attempt to unfold the type and contents of colleaguial relations of professional librarians. In order to understand the type of relationship with their colleagues, we asked the respondents to describe the same in terms of 'formal', 'informal', 'official', ''friendly', etc. The colleague relation has been categorised into two types: informal-equalitarian and bureaucratic-authoritarian. If interaction with the colleagues is confined to formal or official level, we conceptualised it as bureaucratic authoritarian. If it is expressed as 'informal' or 'friendly' we described it in terms of informal-equalitarian. The distinguishing feature of colleague relation in our study is that the majority of respondents (64.0 per cent) maintain informal-equalitarian relations with their colleagues. However, it was also found that a sizable number of respondents (36.0 per cent) behave in bureaucratic-authoritarian fashion with their colleagues.

An analysis of the colleaguial behaviour in respect of background variables (Table 8.1) reveals that sex and experience have more profound influence on the type of relationship. A greater percentage of women professionals (73.8 per cent) have informal dealings with their colleagues compared to their male colleagues (59.3 per cent). Formal relationship seems to be associated with the advancement of age or experience. Professionals with experience of 21 years or more are less likely to be informal among themselves. This suggests that junior librarians or women professionals are more likely to maintain team spirits in role performance.

The content of colleaguial interaction has been explored in terms of two dimensions: Professional and administrative. The professional dimension has been assessed with the following question: "To what extent do you discuss the professional matters with your colleagues? Responses were recorded on a four-point scale: 'never', 'rarely', 'frequently' and 'most often'. What matter should be considered as 'professional' has been left to the judgement of the respondents.

TABLE 8.1: **Nature of Relationship with Colleagues**

Background of librarians	Relationship		Total
	Formal	Informal	
Six			
Male (N=135)	40.7	59.3	100.0
Female (N=65)	26.2	73.8	100.0
Length of Experience			
Up to 10 years (N=84)	32.1	67.9	100.0
11 to 20 years (N=73)	32.9	67.1	100.0
21 year and above (N=43)	41.8	58.2	100.0
Rank			
Senior Level (N=26)	38.5	61.5	100.0
Middle Level (N=80)	38.7	61.3	100.0
Junior Level (N=94)	32.9	67.1	100.0

The findings reveal that majority of respondents (66.5 per cent) had professional discussions with their colleagues. However, there were one-third of respondents (33.5 per cent) who did not indulge in discussions with their colleagues on matters of professional interests.

The extent of colleaguial administrative interaction was further explored by asking the following question: "To what extent do you discuss the administrative matters with your colleagues?". The responses were again recorded on a four-point scale, as stated above. The findings revealed that only one-fourth of respondents (26.0 per cent) did not discuss even the administrative matters with their colleagues. The rest (74.0 per cent) hold a great deal of discussion with their colleagues on matters concerning administrative rulers and procedures.

The colleaguial administrative interaction was further explored in relation to some background variables, *viz.*, rank and types of libraries. The data presented in Table 8.2 clearly show that the senior professionals (80.8 per cent) and middle-level superiors (77.8 per cent) in the libraries are more prone to discuss administrative matters with their colleagues than their junior colleagues (69.2 per cent). Since the former group of professionals are mainly responsible for maintaining discipline in organisations, more frequent discussions among themselves are quite understandable. It is expected that they would achieve greater solidarity among themselves because of their greater interaction with the colleagues. On the other hand, juniors are rarely entrusted with the management of libraries, so they interact less with their colleagues in administrative matters.

TABLE 8.2: **To What Extent Respondents Discuss the Administrative Routines and Procedures With the Colleagues (%)**

Background of Librarians	Extent of discussion		Total
	Never and rarely	Frequently and most often	
Rank			
Senior Level (N=26)	19.2	80.8	100.0
Middle Level (N=80)	22.2	77.8	100.0
Junior Level (N=94)	30.8	69.2	100.0
Types of Libraries			
University (N=83)	18.1	81.9	100.0
Public (N=33)	45.5	54.5	100.0
Special (N=84)	26.2	73.8	100.0

Colleaguial interaction has also been analysed in relation to the different library settings. The data suggest that there is a greater extent of interaction among professional colleagues in university libraries (81.9 per cent) than in the special (73.8 per cent) and public libraries (54.5 per cent). The reason for this difference may be due to the internal structure of these settings. As administrative procedures in the public libraries are reported to be more formalised, the professionals there get less opportunity to hold discussions on administrative matters. On the contrary less formalised settings of university and special libraries provide more ground for discussions on administrative rules and procedures to the professionals. Therefore, it may be inferred that more formalised the procedures, lesser the chances of interaction, among professionals in organisation.

It is also important to know whether interpersonal relation among colleagues is characterised by elements of harmony or hostility. For investigating this aspect of relation, we asked the respondents: "Do your colleagues attempt to improve their prospects by adopting some undesirable means in order to gain favours from their superiors?". The responses were recorded on a four-point scale: 'never', 'rarely', 'frequently' and 'most often'. The findings suggest that 23.0 per cent of respondents would never adopt such undesirable practice while 28.5 per cent of them would rarely indulge in such thing. Surprisingly, there are sizable number of respondents (37.5 per cent) who think that their colleagues would not hesitate to adopt unethical means to gain favour from their superiors. The question being sensitive, 11.0 per cent of respondents did not answer it.

To sum up, there are at least one-fourth to one-third of respondents who would not like to interact with their colleagues on professional or administrative matters. Moreover, a sizable group of respondents also perceive that their colleagues would not behave in a desirable manner. Needless to say that the elements of distrust and suspicion among the colleagues are dysfunctional for the growth of professionalism among the librarians.

PROFESSIONAL-CLIENT RELATIONSHIP

In order to understand the professional-client relationship in library profession, it may be known that the majority of professionals in libraries work "behind the screen". It means that they render indirect service to the clients. (Such indirect services include selection and acquisition of documents, technical processing of reading materials, preparation of abstracts, bibliographies, and documentation lists, etc.) It is only in the reference section that professionals get an opportunity – more than at the issue and return counter — to interact with the clients and render direct service to them. Though even in that section, due to the traditional organisational structure of the libraries, very few professionals are assigned to perform reference services. Moreover, it has also been observed that the level of reference service provided to the clients is not considered very professional. Generally reference services are found to be of directional and locational nature. A survey in this regard has clearly indicated that:

> 44.1 per cent queries were directional, 18 per cent locational, 32 per cent ready reference and 5.9 per cent long reference queries.[3]

The point has been further emphasised by Bundy and Wasserman:

In general library situations, that what is requested by or offered to the patron is ordinarily just not complex enough to be considered a professional service.[4]

Generally, a professional has authority over the clients. By virtue of his specialised knowledge and training, he is supposed to offer the clients the best solution to their problems. It is not necessary that the solution suggested to the client would be according to their wishes, but on the other hand, professional's judgements are to be based on the appropriateness of the problem. However, the above situation does not seem to be applicable for the librarian. Goode observes:

> Thus 'serving' the reader means helping him, learning his wishes and satisfying them. This comes dangerously close to the position taken by a minority of librarians, that their duty is to give the people what they want. . . . At present, the librarians has little power over the clients. . . . The client has the right to check out and use the materials of the library even if the librarian believes he cannot use them to advantage. . . .[5]

Asheim[6] thinks that the failure of librarian to prescribe to the clients is due to the absence of a body of knowledge which provides the base for professional judgement. On the other hand, Bundy and Wasserman feel that:

> The willingness to play an inexpert role may well have been reinforced by the fact that the librarian has had some little knowledge about many things but not very genuine understanding of anything.[7]

Thus, librarians play almost mediating roles in relation to the informational problems of their clients. Because of marginal nature of their roles, we made an attempt to investigate the professional-client relationship, through the perceptions of the clients. Clients in this respect are students from five universities included in the sample.

Clients' Perceptions of Role Images of Librarians

Students were asked to indicate three qualities of professional librarians, in order of preference, for which they should be valued. They were also asked to indicate whether these qualities perceived by them ideally are actually possessed by them. Based on perceptions of the clients, a comparison had been drawn between ideal and actual role images of librarians. Further, it was also considered necessary to know, the extent of gap between clients' perceptions of role images of librarians and professionals' own perceptions of their role images. In addition to the above, we also tried to investigate the clients' perceptions of professional competence of librarians.

The data regarding the role images of librarians have been presented in Table 8.3. The majority of clients perceive that an ideal role of a librarian should have client-orientation. Similarly, a great majority of librarians in their ideal role images, also evaluate themselves in terms of client-orientation. In respect of bureaucratic orientation of role, we find that only a small percentage of clients or librarians give value to it. Surprisingly, professional role of librarian is visible only to a minority of clients. However, librarians also do not give much importance to their professional role in their ideal perceptions.

TABLE 8.3: **A Comparison of Role Images of Librarians based on Perceptions of Clients and Librarians (%)**

Nature of role images	Clients' perceptions			Librarians' perceptions		
	Ideal role images	Actual role attributes	Extent of discrepancy	Self image	Organisational image	Extent of discrepancy
(i) Client Orientation	76.8	45.6	–31.2	65.5	38.0	–27.5
(ii) Professional Orientation	8.8	27.2	+18.4	18.5	29.0	+10.5
(iii) Bureaucratic Orientation	14.4	27.2	+12.8	16.0	33.0	+17.0
Total	100.0	100.0		100.0	100.0	

A comparison of the clients' perceptions of ideal and actual role images of librarians indicates that less than half of the clients fail to perceive the role of librarian as client-oriented and more than one-fourth of them find the librarian to be bureaucratic-oriented. However, it is encouraging to note that the remaining percentage of clients have been able to recognise the professional role of librarians.

Thus, clients' perceptions of actual role performance of librarians indicate that there is a sharp decrease in clients orientation and a sharp increase in bureaucratic orientation. In this regard, the extent of similarity between two types of perceptions — clients' perceptions of actual role attributes and librarians' perceptions of organisational role image may be noted. The finding seems to be most significant. It reveals that high client orientation, as perceived by both clients and professionals, suffers a great deal of erosion in the context of organisations. It seems that organisational values do not lay much stress on service-orientation. Rather, we find that organisational values tend to minimise the service orientation and provide support to bureaucratic orientation. As such, organisations would not be able to meet the expectations of the clients. In such circumstances professionals would also have to strive hard in preserving client orientation in order to meet the competing demands of the organisations.

It would not be out of place to mention some of the comments expressed by the clients in respect of the actual role attributes of librarians. These comments or opinions high-light the bureaucratic elements in librarians' role performance:

(i) "Librarians do not try to understand the problems of the clients. Most of the time they are not aware of their work also."
(ii) "Librarians remain busy with official business and they have little time for the users."
(iii) "Librarians are stickers for rules and are not very cooperative in dealing with their clients. They think that library rules are not meant for providing convenience to the students."
(iv) "In general, librarians are not accessible to the clients and they do not find enough time to solve the problem of the clients."
(v) "As librarians remain busy in unnecessary things, so they direct most of their work to their subordinates who also do not take interest in work."
(vi) "Librarians do not have helpful attitude towards users, rather they try to avoid situations in which users could be helped."
(vii) "There is nothing worth mentioning about librarians, except that they are ignorant and are more concerned about their duty hours."
(viii) "Librarians often fail to appreciate the genuine problem of the users. They take little interest in the students' problems."

(ix) "Librarians work in their own way, ignoring the problem of the clients."

(x) "Librarians seem to be disinterested in the job. If they help some users, they make the users feel as if they are put under an obligation.

The above opinions expressed by the clients further strengthen the contention that librarians set store more by bureaucratic rules and regulations than by client orientations. Thus, expectations of the majority of clients remain unfulfilled and as a result of that several clients hold many unfavourable images of librarians. Librarians are often described by them as 'rough', 'rude', 'indifferent', 'uncooperative', 'irritated', 'ill-behaved', 'insensitive to innovation', etc.

Expert Role of Professionals

As discussed, generally professionals are recognised for performing expert's role in relation to their clients. However, the same situation does not seem to apply in the case of librarians at present. While majority of clients expect that librarians should have high academic and professional qualifications, they are not convinced that professionals can provide specialised information service to them. A large number of students (67.2 per cent) do not consider librarians to be subject-experts. However, they think that librarians are good enough for providing general guidance to the users.

The question arises as to why the clients hold such negative perceptions about the librarians? One of the reasons behind such perceptions could probably be that majority of the clients lack direct contact with the librarians and they are not aware of their professional roles. When they were asked to indicate whether they usually sought help from a reference librarian, it was revealed that only 18.4 per cent of them came in constant touch ('frequently' and 'always') with the professional librarian, while 74.4 per cent of them sought help only 'sometimes'. The remaining 7.2 per cent did not take any help from the librarian. When asked to state whether their interaction with a librarian was a learning experience, that 19.2 per cent of the student had 'frequently' or 'always' found it so, while more 52.0 per cent experienced it only 'sometimes'. It is also significant to note that 28.8 per cent of the students did not find any opportunity to interact with the librarians. Thus, it may be emphasised that the existing organisation of professional role activities in libraries do not provide much opportunity to the professionals for making direct contact with the clients. Generally clients interact with other categories of library personnel who do not possess required professional knowledge for understanding their problems. As such, professionals usually fail to project their appropriate role image.

NOTES

1. S.R. Ranganathan (1948), *Preface to Library Science*, Delhi: University of Delhi, pp. 95-96.
2. *Ibid.*
3. St. Clair, Jeffrey and Aluri Rao (1977), "Staffing the Reference Desk: Professional of Non-professionals", *Journal of Academic Administration*, Vol. 3, pp. 149-53.
4. Mary Lee Bundy and Paul Wasserman (1968), "Professionalism Reconsidered", *College and Research Libraries*, Vol. 29, pp. 5-26.
5. William J. Goode (1962), "The Librarian : From Occupation to Profession", in Philip H. Ennis and Howard W. Winger (eds.), *Seven Questions About the Profession of Librarianship*, Chicago, The University of Chicago, pp. 8-22.
6. Lester Asheim (1979), "Librarians as Professionals", *Library Trends*, Vol. 27, pp. 225-57.
7. Bundy and Wasserman (1968), op. cit.

NINE

BUREAUCRATISATION AND PROFESSIONALISATION: THEIR INTERRELATIONSHIP IN THE CASE OF LIBRARIANSHIP

THE METHODOLOGICAL assumption that both bureaucracy and profession stand on divergent principles, and yet share some common characteristics was noted in Chapter one. This chapter examines the degree of bureaucratisation and professionalisation, as perceived by librarians in course of their role performance in varying organisational contexts and to how far they are affected by these contradictory processes.

BUREAUCRATIC DIMENSIONS

Max Weber's analysis of bureaucracy as an administrative institution continues to be regarded as classic. According to Weber,[1] bureaucracy exhibits a large number of characteristics, viz., hierarchy of authority, systematic division of labour, technical competence, impersonality, etc. He visualised bureaucracy as an 'ideal type', that is, no actual organisation is bureaucratic in the strict sense of his definition. After Weber, several social scientists have studied the bureaucracy and tried to delimit or subdivide the characteristics. Hall,[2] has made an attempt to present all such characteristics used by several authors in their studies of formal organisation (Table 9.1).

Blau[3] lists four basic characteristics of bureaucratic form of organisation as (a) a clear-cut hierarchy of authority; (b) specialisation; (c) a clearly detailed system of rules and (d) impersonality in allocating and co-ordinating rules. The first three characteristics are 'structural' while the fourth characteristics is 'behavioural' since it involves decisional matters. Based on Weberian concept, the structural characteristics of bureaucracy which help us in understanding the organisational structure are often referred to as centralisation (i.e. hierarchy of authority), specialisation, or complexity (i.e. division of labour) and formalisation (i.e. system of rules) in organisational literature.[4]

DIMENSIONAL APPROACH

Bureaucracy can be studied as a total phenomenon. It can also be approached by separating it into dimensions. Hall[5] suggests that dimensional approach would be more fruitful because it may indicate the degree of bureaucratisation on each of the dimensions studied. It may further provide an added advantage of combining scores of various subdimensions to form a cumulative scale of bureaucracy.[6]

Three structural dimensions of bureaucracy, viz., centralisation, specialisation and formalisation as mentioned above, were chosen for investigating the degree of bureaucratisation in the various types of libraries of Delhi. It may be noted that in the ideal-type bureaucracy one could expect that all of the three dimensions would be present to a high degree, while non-bureaucratic or simple organisation would have low degree of these dimensions. For measurement of each of these dimensions indices were constructed. Items used for making these indices are discussed separately in Appendices III, IV, V. Attempt was also made to assess the overall bureaucratisation by combining the scores of all three dimensions. Table 9.2 shows the distribution of librarians on these three dimensions employed in the research.

It is evident from Table 9.2 that all dimensions of bureaucracy are not on the higher side in library organisations. In respect of two dimensions, viz., centralisation of decision-making and formalisation, library organisations seem to be highly bureaucratised while they are quite low so far as specialisation is concerned. Forty-five per cent of respondents perceive lower degree of specialisation in the libraries. This suggests that professional roles in libraries are not clearly demarcated or defined and most of the professionals remain engaged in mainly nonprofessional or semi-professional activities. The absence of specialised role in libraries raises the likelihood of the emergence of more routine activities that would necessarily be controlled or closely supervised by a centralised hierarchy or more rigid system of rules. Thus, it may be understood that the lack of differentiation of functions may accentuate the degree of centralisation.

TABLE 9.1: **Characteristics of Bureaucracy as Listed by Major Authors**

Dimensions of bureaucracy	Weber	Friedrich	Merton	Udy	Heady	Parsons	Berger	Michel	Dimock
Hierarchy of authority	*	*	*	*	*	*	*	*	*
Division of labour . . .	*	*	*	*	*	*	-	*	*
Technically competent participants . . .	*	*	*	*	-	*	*	-	-
Procedural devices for work situations	*	*	*	-	*	-	*	-	*
Rules governing behaviour or positional incumbents	*	*	*	-	-	-	*	*	-
Limited Authority of office	*	-	*	-	*	*	-	-	-
Differential rewards by office	*	-	-	*	-	-	-	-	-
Impersonality of personal contact	-	-	*	-	-	-	-	-	-
Administration separate from ownership	*	-	-	-	-	-	-	-	-
Emphasis on written communication	*	-	-	-	-	-	-	-	-
Rational discipline	*	-	-	-	-	-	-	-	-

* Cited by author.

Source: Richard H. Hall (1963), "The Concept of Bureaucracy", *American Journal of Sociology*, Vol. 59, pp. 32-40.

TABLE 9.2: **Ratings of Respondents on Bureaucratic Characteristics (Percentage)**

Bureaucratic characteristics	Rating (N = 200)			Total
	High	Moderate	Low	
Centralisation	47.0	25.3	27.7	100.00
Specialisation	21.0	34.0	45.0	100.0
Formalisation	46.5	27.0	26.5	100.0
Overall Bureaucratisation	49.0	30.8	20.2	100.0

BUREAUCRATIC DIMENSIONS BY BACKGROUND CHARACTERISTICS

Bureaucratic dimensions, as perceived by the male and female respondents, have been presented in Table 9.3. A higher percentage of female librarians think that there is high concentration of centralisation of decision-making authority in the libraries. It indicates that women librarians are less involved in the decision-making. As power of decision-making in the organisations is concentrated in the hands of few seniors who happen to be males, female members are likely to perceive higher degree of centralisation. Lack of participation in the decision making process by the women librarians seems to be the result of their placement on the junior levels.

Women librarians perceive higher degree of specialisation in the libraries as compared to the male librarians. As the jobs assigned to the female librarians are mostly of technical nature, e.g. classification, cataloguing, indexing, etc. they consider their roles more specialised. On the contrary, the roles assigned to male librarians mostly relate to the administrative work. Consequently they are less likely to perceive their work as specialised. More involvement of male librarians in the bureaucratic roles also necessiate them to observe rules and regulation of the organisations more strictly so they are likely to perceive higher degree of formalisation in libraries. On the contrary the role-situations of female librarians are less administrative, so comparatively lower percentage of them would consider formalisation (31.5 per cent) as high.

The study does not reveal any influence of professional qualifications on the dimensions of bureaucracy (Table 9.4). The assumption that higher professional qualifications may increase the degree of specialisation in the organisations is not borne out by the study.

TABLE 9.3: **Bureaucratic Dimensions by Sex (%)**

Dimensions of bureaucracy		Sex	
		Male (N = 135)	Female (N = 65)
Centralisation			
	High	42.5	56.3
	Moderate	24.6	56.3
	Low	32.9	17.2
	Total	100.0	100.0
Specialisation			
	High	17.8	27.7
	Moderate	38.5	24.6
	Low	43.7	47.7
	Total	100.0	100.0
Formalisation			
	High	50.4	38.5
	Moderate	26.6	27.7
	Low	23.0	33.8
	Total	100.0	100.0

The findings regarding the degree of bureaucratisation in relation to the hierarchical positions of respondents are presented in Table 9.5. The data suggest that junior librarians consider their work-organisations as highly centralised. It seems that only senior (36.0 per cent) and middle level (37.5 per cent) librarians are participating in the decision-making process.

In terms of specialisation of function, it is clear that a sizable group of librarians in all ranks show low level of specialisation. It is also clear that lower percentage of senior librarians perceive higher degree of specialisation in libraries. It seems that as seniors are involved mostly in the administrative functions, so they perceive lower degree of specialisation.

Regarding formalisation, it may be noticed that both junior and middle level librarians almost equally perceive higher degree of formalisation in libraries. As senior members of the organisations are entrusted with some discretionary powers in order to take some *ad hoc* decisions, so they have lower proportions on the higher degree of formalisation as compared to the middle (48.8 per cent) and junior level librarians (47.9 per cent).

TABLE 9.4: **Bureaucratic Dimensions by Respondents' Professional Qualifications (%)**

Dimensions of bureaucracy		Professional Qualifications	
		Higher (N = 76)	Minimum (N = 124)
Centralisation			
	High	41.9	50.0
	Moderate	24.3	25.8
	Low	33.8	24.2
	Total	100.0	100.0
Specialisation			
	High	18.4	22.6
	Moderate	35.5	33.1
	Low	46.1	44.3
	Total	100.0	100.0
Formalisation			
	High	44.8	47.6
	Moderate	27.6	26.7
	Low	27.6	25.7
	Total	100.0	100.0

Bureaucratisation has also been examined in relation to the different types of libraries, viz., university, public and special (see Table 9.6). Higher degree of centralisation may be noticed in the case of university and public libraries. But special libraries are characterised by lesser degree of centralisation. It may perhaps be so because specialisation presupposes technical competence and some amount of freedom in decision-making.

The data do not support that specialisation operates satisfactorily in any of the above types of libraries. However, the degree of specialisation is quite low in the case of public libraries as compared to the university and special libraries. It seems that the presence of such factors as lack of distinction between professional and non-professional tasks and lack of adequate number of professional staff (in relation to the total population of the clients) do not provide sufficient opportunity for specialisation.

TABLE 9.5: **Bureaucratic Dimensions by Respondents' Positions in Organisations (%)**

Dimensions of bureaucracy		Rank		
		Senior (N=26)	Middle (N=80)	Junior (N=94)
Centralisation				
	High	36.0	37.5	58.1
	Moderate	24.0	28.7	22.6
	Low	40.0	33.8	19.3
	Total	100.0	100.0	100.0
Specialisation				
	High	11.5	23.7	21.3
	Moderate	46.2	26.3	37.2
	Low	42.3	50.0	41.5
	Total	100.0	100.0	100.0
Formalisation				
	High	34.6	48.8	47.9
	Moderate	42.3	21.2	27.7
	Low	23.1	30.0	24.4
	Total	100.0	100.0	100.0

Organisations which generally perform non-professional tasks are likely to be centralised. Role occupants in such organisations need an elaborate system of rules and regulations for guidance. Our data suggest that almost all types of libraries exhibit higher degree of formalisation. However, public libraries are more formalised (57.6 per cent) as compared to the special (40.5 per cent) and university (48.2 per cent) libraries. Perhaps this may be so due to the fact that public libraries follow the pattern of government organisations which have a long tradition of established system of formalised rules. Contrary to the former, special libraries indicate somewhat lower degree of formalisation. It may be inferred that since special libraries deal with only limited number of clients who happen to be members of their own organisations, rules are more conveniently relaxed in their favour. But the university libraries, which deal with a large number of clients who need to be dealt with uniformally, are more formalised as compared to the special libraries.

TABLE 9.6: **Bureaucratic Dimensions by Types of Libraries (percentage)**

Dimensions of bureaucracy		Types of Libraries		
		University (N = 83)	Public (N = 33)	Special (N = 84)
Centralisation				
	High	51.2	51.5	41.0
	Moderate	25.6	18.2	27.7
	Low	23.2	30.3	31.3
	Total	100.0	100.0	100.0
Specialisation				
	High	22.9	21.2	19.1
	Moderate	37.3	27.3	33.3
	Low	39.8	51.5	47.6
	Total	100.0	100.0	100.0
Formalisation				
	High	48.2	57.6	40.5
	Moderate	27.7	21.2	28.5
	Low	24.1	21.2	31.0
	Total	100.0	100.0	100.0

PROFESSIONAL DIMENSIONS

Attributes of a profession have been described in Chapter One. These attributes are mainly of two types. The first type of attributes relates to the structure of the occupation. Such structural attributes include the creation of a full time occupation, the establishment of a training school, formation of a professional association and a code of ethics. The second type of attributes is attitudinal. These attributes reveal the attitude and behaviour of the practitioners such as sense of calling to the field, feeling of autonomy, desire for strong colleague relationship, etc. Hall[7] had made use of the following attitudinal dimensions in his study of professionalism. These are: (a) use of professional organisation as a major referent; (b) belief in service to the public; (c) belief in self-regulation; (d) sense of calling to the field and (e) autonomy. In this study the following attitudinal components have been utilised for examining the extent of professionalisation among librarians of Delhi: (a) commitment to professional orientations; (b) Client orientation and (c) work related autonomy and utilisation of professional knowledge and skill.

COMMITMENT TO PROFESSIONAL ORIENTATIONS

Formal or informal professional associations play a major role in the lives of the professionals. They reinforce the values, beliefs and identity of the profession. Gross[8] indicated that by attending professional meetings and by reading professional journals, practitioners develop "colleague consciousness". In course of time they become influenced by the standards of the profession and as a result they develop commitment to the profession.

CLIENT ORIENTATION

The chief concern of a professional is to serve his clients. He believes that his profession is indispensable and beneficial to society. Clients, thus, constitute an important element both for profession and bureaucracy. While a professional is expected to maintain personal relationship with the client, an organisational man indirectly looks after the general interests of the clients. But clients' interests remain supreme in both the cases. Specially in a service organisation, the collective interests of the clients are not to be allowed to lose sight of for the sake of maintaining bureaucratic procedures. Therefore, the degree to which professionals are oriented towards the service of the clients may be considered as an important component for measuring professionalism.

WORK-RELATED AUTONOMY AND UTILISATION OF PROFESSIONAL KNOWLEDGE AND SKILL

Professional autonomy is the most critical component of professionalisation. It may exist at two separate but related levels: (a) with respect to the individual professional and (b) with respect to the profession.[9] The former aspect is the subject of investigation of this study. Autonomy in the context would mean that a professional is free to take decisions about his work. He should conduct the service according to the needs of the clients. He is allowed to formulate his own strategy keeping in view the standards of his professional knowledge and training. His decisions regarding the client's service should not be influenced by the threat of organisational practices. The loss of such work-related autonomy to the professional would mean that quality of clients' service would be reduced and professionals would not be allowed to innovate or initiate changes according to the specific problems of the clients.

For assessment of the above dimensions of professionalisation, indices were constructed. One of the dimensions of profession, i.e., *Commitment to Professional Orientation* was examined in Chapter Six. Items used for measuring the other two dimensions, viz., *Client Orientation* and *Work-related Autonomy* were provided in Appendix VI and VII of this chapter. Table 9.7 presents the distribution of respondents on all three dimensions.

TABLE 9.7: **Ratings of Respondents on Professional Dimensions (%)**

Professional characteristics	Rating (N = 200)			Total
	High	Moderate	Low	
Commitment to Professional Orientations	35.5	32.0	32.5	100.0
Client-Orientation	42.2	37.7	20.1	100.0
Work-related Autonomy	31.0	50.5	18.5	100.0
Overall Professionalisation	42.2	25.6	32.2	100.0

One of the striking features one could notice from the above table is that professionals do not enjoy a great deal of work-related autonomy. Less than one-third of the respondents (31.0 per cent) perceive higher degree of autonomy while half of them (50.5 per cent) perceive only moderate degree of autonomy in their libraries. Similar is the pattern we find in the case of another dimension of professionalisation, i.e., Commitment to Professional Orientations. Nearly two-thirds of the respondents show low to moderate degree of professional commitments, while slightly more than one-third of them (35.5 per cent) indicate high commitment to professional orientations. However, a large percentage of respondents are disposed to client orientation (42.2 per cent). It may be recalled that while investigating the role image of respondents, it was observed that 38.0 per cent of them had indicated client orientations in their organisational role images. This is indicative of the fact that respondents seem to be more or less consistent in their perceptions.

Professional dimensions have also been examined in relation to respondents' background variables. As an investigation in respect of commitment to professional orientations was made earlier (Chapter Six) we would concentrate here only on the remaining two other dimensions, viz., client orientation and work-related autonomy. While client orientation is not found to be influenced by any background variables, it may be stated that the respondents perceptions regarding autonomy are likely to be influenced by some of the background variables (Table 9.8). The data suggest that compared to the men, women in the profession are likely to perceive less autonomy in their sphere of work. It means that they require more supervision. It seems that the superiors in the organisations are free to make decisions regarding their plans and procedures. This shows that they might be providing guidelines to the majority of middle level and junior librarians. Consequently, only a minority among junior librarians (19.1 per cent) and a little more than one-third of middle level librarians perceive higher degree of autonomy in their work situations. It is obvious that work would be highly routinised for majority of public librarians (66.6 per cent) who perceive moderate autonomy. Only a small section of public librarians who are in higher ranks enjoy a higher degree of autonomy. We also do not find conclusive evidence to suggest that special librarians are more prone to innovative practices.

Respondents have been further examined in respect of overall professionalisation (it has been measured by combining the score of each attitudinal dimensions of the profession as indicated in Table 9.7). An investigation into overall professionalisation of respondents in respect of their background variables shows (Table 9.9) that the proportion of women librarians indicating low level of professionalisation is higher (45.3 per cent) as compared to their male counterparts (25.9 per cent). Needless to mention that in the case of women, lower professionalism is the result of their dual roles and their placements in organisational hierarchies.

TABLE 9.8: **Work Autonomy by Background Characteristics (%)**

Background characteristics	Ranking of respondents			Total
	High	Moderate	Low	
Sex				
Male (N = 135)	33.3	51.9	14.8	100.0
Female (N = 65)	26.2	47.6	26.2	100.0
Ranks				
Senior (N = 26_	61.5	38.5	0.0	100.0
Middle (N = 80)	35.0	53.8	11.2	100.0
Junior (N = 94)	19.1	51.1	29.8	100.0
Types of Libraries				
University (N=83)	31.3	49.4	19.3	100.0
Public (N=33)	18.2	66.6	15.2	100.0
Special (N-84)	35.7	45.2	19.1	100.0

The data shown in Table 9.9 suggest that higher level of professionalism is greatly associated with higher professional ranks and higher achievements in profession. It may be noticed that one-fourth of junior librarians are placed high on the dimension of professionalisation while less than half of them indicate lower level of professionalism.

In the case of middle level librarians, contrary to their junior colleagues, we find that half of them indicate higher degree of professionalisation while overwhelming majority of their seniors are placed on high dimension of professionalism. Organisational milieu of librarians does not make much difference in their degrees of professionalisation. However, public librarians show slightly lower level of professionalisation.

INTER-RELATIONS BETWEEN BUREAUCRATISATION AND PROFESSIONALISATION

The co-existence of bureaucracy and professionalism is the characteristic of the service organisations, like libraries. Professionals in such organisations hold both these values together. But in order to examine the inter-relationship between professionalisation and bureaucratisation, an attempt was made to analyse the three characteristics of professionalisation with the overall scale of bureaucratisation (Tables 9.10, 9.11 and 9.12).

TABLE 9.9: **Overall Professionalisation by Background Variables (%)**

Background characteristics	Ranking of respondents			Total
	High	Moderate	Low	
Sex				
Male (N=135)	47.4	26.7	25.9	100.0
Female (N=63)	31.3	23.4	45.3	100.0
Professional Qualification				
Higher (N=76)	51.3	25.0	23.7	100.0
Minimum (N=124)	36.3	26.3	37.4	100.0
Rank				
Seniors (N=26)	76.9	15.4	7.7	100.0
Middle (N=80)	50.0	25.0	25.0	100.0
Juniors (N=94)	25.8	29.0	45.2	100.0
Types of Libraries				
University (N=83)	41.0	25.3	33.7	100.0
Public (N=33)	36.4	33.3	30.3	100.0
Special (N=64)	45.8	22.9	31.3	100.0

TABLE 9.10: **Commitment to Professional Orientations and Bureaucratisation (%)**

Bureaucratisation	Commitment to professional orientation			Total
	High	Moderate	Low	
High (N=97)	22.7	27.8	49.5	100.0
Moderate (N=63)	38.1	42.9	19.0	100.0
Low (N=40)	62.5	27.5	10.0	100.0

The bureaucratic process in libraries greatly affects individuals' commitments towards professional orientations (Table 9.10). A great majority of respondents (62.5 per cent), who are placed low on the scale of bureaucratisation, show high professional commitments. The same aspect may be further highlighted by observing the respondents on high scale of bureaucratisation. It may be noticed that only less than one-fourth of respondents (22.7 per cent) placed high on the bureaucratisation scale show high commitment to professional orientations, while nearly fifty per cent of the respondents placed on the same scale indicate low professional commitment. Therefore, it may be suggested that higher the bureaucratisation in the libraries, lower the commitment towards professional orientations.

TABLE 9.11: **Work Autonomy and Bureaucratisation**

Bureaucratisation	Work autonomy			Total
	High	Moderate	Low	
High (N=97)	28.9	49.5	21.6	100.0
Moderate (N=63)	23.8	52.3	23.9	100.0
Low (N=40)	47.5	50.5	2.5	100.0

TABLE 9.12: **Client Orientations and Bureaucratisation (%)**

Bureaucratisation	Client orientations			Total
	High	Moderate	Low	
High (N=97)	42.3	46.4	11.3	100.0
Moderate (N=63)	36.5	34.9	28.6	100.0
Low (N=40)	45.0	27.5	27.5	100.0

Another professional dimension which is affected by the process of bureaucratisation is autonomy (Table 9.11). Desire to innovate and chances of utilisation of professional skills seem to be bleak in libraries. It may be noticed that slightly more than one-fourth of respondents (28.9 per cent) placed high on the dimension of bureaucracy, enjoy only high autonomy in the libraries. Conversely, nearly half of the respondents who perceive low bureaucratisation are placed high on the dimension of autonomy. Therefore, it is indicated that lower the bureaucratisation, higher the autonomy.

In respect of client orientations, it may be observed that high client orientations may exist among both types of professionals — either placed high (42.7 per cent) or placed low on the scale of bureaucratisation (45.0 per cent). It means that professionals are likely to preserve client orientation in all types of libraries irrespective of their being highly bureaucratised or highly professionalised.

In nutshell, both bureaucratisation and professionalisation are the inevitable processes for the organisational professionals. But bureaucratic dimensions loom large on the process of professionalisation. Specially the lower level of specialisation inhibits the growth of professionalisation. Besides this, other two dimensions of professionalisation, *viz.*, commitment to professional orientations and autonomy are also seriously impaired by the bureaucratic process. However, client orientation remains predominant irrespective of these processes.

NOTES

1. Max Weber (1946), *From Max Weber: Essays in Sociology, eds. Hans H. Gerth and C. Wright Mills, London, Oxford University Press, pp. 196-244.*
2. *Richard H. Hall (1963), "The Concept of Bureaucracy"* American Journal of Sociology, *Vol.59, pp. 32-40.*
3. *See Everett K. Wilson (1966),* Sociology: Rules, Roles and Relationships, *Homeland, Illinois, The Dorsey Press (1956), pp. 525. See also Peter M. Blau, 1956 Bureaucracy in Modern Society (1956),* New York: Random House.
4. Curt Tausky (1983), "Formal Organisation", in Robert Hagedorm, *Sociology*, Dubuque, Iowa, Wm.C. Brown, p. 476.
5. Richard H. Hall (1963), op. cit., p. 33.
6. See Rechard H. Hall and Charles R. Tittle (1966-67), "A Note on Bureaucracy and Its Correlates," *American Journal of Sociology,* Vol.72, pp. 267-72.
7. See Richard H. Hall (1968), "Professionalisation and Bureaucratisation," *American Sociological Review,* Vol.33, pp. 92-121.
8. Edward A. Gross (1958), *Work and Society,* New York, Thomas Y. Crowell.
9. See, Gloria V. Engel (1970), "Professional Autonomy and Bureaucratic Organisation", *Administrative Science Quarterly,* Vol. 15, pp. 12-21.

TEN

SUMMING-UP

THE PROBLEM

Professions and bureaucracy are regarded as irreconcilable systems. Therefore, it has been hypothesised by several researchers that professionals would face many dilemmas while working in organisations. Understandably, consequences of bureaucratisation for professions have attracted the attention of many social scientists.

Given the changed ''work-ecology' of professionals, both full-fledged professions and semi-professions have become organisation based. However, members of several full-fledged professions have a dual work-situation: some practise independently while others work in organisations. On the other hand, most semi-professions are invariably practised in organisations. So the important point for consideration in the case of semi-professions is how far the degree of professionalisation gets affected when these are practised in organisations. In this regard, it may be argued that some of the consequences which have been found to be applicable for the full-fledged professions may not be valid for the majority of semi-professions. It may further be argued that there would be varying consequences for each type of semi-professions depending upon their degree of professionalisation and work-milieu. The present work is an attempt to study one type of organisational professionals, i.e., trained librarians working in different types of libraries. Thus, one of the major tasks of the present study was to investigate the elements of professionalisation and bureaucratisation and their inter-relationship in varying organisational contexts in which librarians perform their roles.

Librarianship emerged in India during the past fifty years. During its brief history the profession has made significant progress in relation to professional education, professional organisation and clientele services, besides defining its role and status in a developing society like India. But little is known about librarians from a sociological point of view.

To fill in this gap the study attempted to explore the following aspects of the library professionals in their:

(1) socio-economic backgrounds;
(2) occupational careers in terms of (a) motivational orientations for the choice of occupation; (b) sources of communication for occupational choice; (c) career mobility and (d) occupational prestige.
(3) role commitments, role perceptions and role obligations;
(4) role images and value orientations;
(5) role relations in terms of superior-subordinate relations, colleaguial relations and professional-client relations and
(6) extent of perceptions of bureaucratisation and professionalisation in library organisations.

UNIVERSE OF STUDY

Delhi which has nearly 15 per cent of the total libraries and 10 per cent of the total population of librarians in India was selected for the present study. For collection of data a sample of 200 trained librarians from 5 university libraries, 2 public libraries and 15 special libraries were taken. On the basis of their positions and salary-structures, librarians were grouped into three categories: senior, middle and understandably the largest group, junior.

The bulk of the data were collected through structured questionnaires in 1985. The response rate was 67.2 per cent. Barring factual information most other data collected from them were behavioural or perceptual at the cognitive level. Data from a select group of users were also collected for ascertaining their understanding of the role of librarians. The collected data were coded, computer-processed and analysed to yield the various inferences/results.

SOCIO-ECONOMIC BACKGROUND OF LIBRARIANS

Owing to the close relationship between social structure and occupation, socio-economic background of librarians was studied in order to investigate the recruitment base of the profession. Besides obtaining information on personal and organisational attributes of librarians, a detailed analysis of background factors such as religion, caste, linguistic-region, rural-urban background etc., was made. A study of the family background of librarians was also considered necessary in order to know the extent of social mobility which librarians might have experienced in their careers.

An analysis of sex-composition of library professionals reveals that majority of librarians are men. The population of women librarians constitute only one-third of the total population of librarians.

Librarianship is a female dominated profession in the industrialised countries. Women are generally found to be heavily concentrated in semi-professions such as nursing, school-teaching, social-work and librarianship. Their low representation in high status professions is well-known. In India, the representation of women in organised sector is relatively low due to certain historical reasons. Besides nursing, women are largely concentrated in school teaching.

Our findings indicate that librarianship is the second most favourite profession for women in India, though this trend is relatively new. The three-fold increase in the population of women librarians within two decades between sixties and eighties gives us an indication that in future more women would be inclined to take up jobs in libraries. The leading factors contributing to this process are, increased facilities of library education, growing number of libraries in urban centres and favourable social attitude towards librarianship as a suitable occupation for women. If the same trend continues, which is not unlikely, feminisation of library profession in India is possible.

Librarians of Delhi are mainly drawn from upper caste, urban Hindu families of North India. However, it is also interesting to note that almost all the major religious communities and all the major linguistic-regional groups are more or less proportionately represented in the profession.

The dominance of upper castes is very visible in all modern professions in India. Our findings indicated that two-thirds of librarians were from the three twice-born *varnas*. Only less than one-third of them belonged to intermediate castes which constitute the bulk of the population. However, librarians from the Scheduled Castes constituted 10.2 per cent. The low representation of the members of intermediate castes in the profession seems to be the consequence of their social and educational backwardness. However, in the case of Scheduled Castes we find that the policy of reservation pursued by the Government has shown encouraging results, although their representation in prestigious professions such as medicine, engineering and college teaching is still very limited. Their better representation in librarianship as compared to other prestigious professions may be due to its relatively low competitive character.

Women librarians are drawn mainly from upper castes and only a small percentage of them (17 per cent) belong to intermediate and lower castes. This shows that professional education has not gained adequate acceptability among intermediate and lower castes and as such the educational opportunities and other facilities are mostly utilised by the male members of these castes.

Librarians of Delhi are predominantly from Hindi speaking States of North India. In our sample 42 per cent belong to Delhi and the remaining 58 per cent are first generation migrants from other States. Sex-wise inter-regional mobility indicates that nearly two-thirds of the men librarians are from outside Delhi while less than one-third of women librarians are migrants from other States. Understandably, the location of their husbands' jobs and familial responsibility hinder women's mobility.

The general trend in professions is to attract people from urban centres and librarianship is not an exception. Majority of librarians had urban or semi-urban upbringing and only one-fourth of them had rural background. With the exception of one librarian who had rural upbringing all the women professionals grew up in urban environment. Needless to say, due to lack of proper facilities in rural areas women are relatively insulated from professional education and are deprived of economic independence through jobs.

The data regarding inter-generational educational mobility reveal that librarians are an educationally upward mobile group. The overwhelming majority of librarians are more educated than their fathers. Only a negligible percentage of them are less educated than their fathers while one-fifth of them are equally educated.

The fathers of women librarians were better educated than the fathers of men librarians. It is important to note that fathers of lower castes librarians were illiterate or only school educated. In the case of librarians from the intermediate castes, nearly half of their fathers had also the same level of education. This shows the close relationship between caste and education.

An analysis of occupational background of librarians' fathers indicate that the recruitment in the profession is mainly from urban-based occupations which shows only intrastratum mobility. The mobility across the stratum accounts for only 37 per cent (*i.e.*, 18 per cent of librarians' fathers were in agriculture and 19 per cent were in business). In the set of urban occupations, white-collar groups alone supply as much as 40 per cent of the librarians and the contribution of the urban professional classes account for less than 15 per cent. Thus, the occupational base of librarianship seems to be the sons and daughters of men of lower administrative services than that of higher administrative services and professional classes.

Considering the economic status of librarians' fathers, we find that the overwhelming majority of librarians were recruited from the lower middle group or lower strata of the society. Only a negligible percentage of them considered their fathers to be economically well-off. Women librarians were, however, from somewhat well-off families. In this respect the recruitment base of librarians shows similarity to that of the school teachers, a semi-professional occupation.

OCCUPATIONAL CAREER

For the choice of an occupation, members of a community should have information about the occupation they want to choose. A substantial number of librarians were influenced by inter-personal network. The influence of mass media, in this respect, was negligible.

Majority of librarians had either utilitarian orientation behind the choice of profession or drifted into the profession by chance. More than half of the librarians were working as clerks, school teachers and temporary college teachers before they made the final decision to opt for librarianship. Obviously, less advantageous economic background forced them to have utilitarian consideration for the choice of occupation. Only a negligible percentage of the sample had alturistic motive in choosing the career.

One-third of the librarians had 'immobile' career in the profession. Upward mobility in the career had been experienced by less than half of the professionals, whose nature of mobility involved inter-organisational movement. The direction of inter-organisational movements shows that librarians generally move from low-status, low paid organisations to high-status, high-paid organisations. Only a small percentage of librarians were fortunate enough — men more so than women — to experience upward mobility in their career through promotions in the same organisation where they joined initially.

A majority of librarians equated their profession with school teaching, one-third of them also considered it at par with subordinate administrative jobs. The implication of this self-rating is that librarians equipped with high academic training and professional knowledge are likely to suffer from prestige deprivation.

While the majority of librarians were satisfied with their career it is also important to note that more than one-third of them were dissatisfied with it. Women librarians enjoyed higher-degree of satisfaction. The reasons for this, seem to be their 'non-careerist' orientation and the fact that they are subsidiary bread winners in the family. Because of the high job expectations young librarians are prone to inter-regional and inter-organisational mobility. The spatial mobility facilitates upward career mobility which gives them satisfaction in their career. This is in contrast to experienced professionals whose dissatisfaction may be located in their self-imposed restrictions on inter-organisational mobility and consequent career immobility in the present organisations. A section of librarians, who adopted the para-professional route of entry into the occupation, seemed satisfied because of their upward mobility in the career. Better working conditions and salary-structure made a career more satisfying in university and special libraries than in public libraries.

ROLE STRUCTURE

The role structure of librarians is examined in terms of their role commitment, perception, obligation and images.

Role commitment of librarians was examined from two dimensions: (a) Role commitment in regard to occupation as a whole, and (b) Content of commitment. The first dimension presents the instrumental perspective of role commitment and the second one covers the professional perspective.

Majority of the librarians are only instrumentally committed to their roles. Weak commitments to roles have been reported only by one-fourth of librarians. In spite of high role commitment (in this direction) majority of librarians would not influence the occupational career of their offsprings in favour of library profession because of its low prestige in the society. Understandably, librarians hold high aspirations about their children and would like to see them in some more prestigious professions.

In regard to the second dimension of commitment, we do not find that librarians are highly attached to professional activities. High professional content of commitment was indicated by slightly more than one-third of respondents only. Professional content of commitment was found lower in the case of women professionals, most probably because of their dual roles. Higher professional qualifications, higher ranks in organisation and upward mobility tend to increase the professional content of commitments. Special and university librarians have shown higher degree of role commitment, perhaps, because their work-settings are more professionalised.

Role perceptions of librarians was assessed through 'self-perception of roles' and 'perception of colleagues' role in terms of bureaucratic, professional and client orientations. In regard to the self-role perceptions librarians are found to be equally distributed on professional and client orientations. Only a few respondents tended to be bureaucratic in orientation. But taking cognisance of the perceptions of their colleagues' role for the same dimension, it was found that the extent of discrepancy in regard to the above role orientations is substantial. Nearly half of the librarians attributed bureaucratic role orientations to their colleagues. The findings in respect of client orientation is rather disturbing. While 46 per cent of librarians perceived their 'self-role' to be client oriented, surprisingly only half of them would attribute the same role orientation to their colleagues. However, in the case of professional orientation, there is less gap between 'self-perception of roles' and 'perception of colleagues role'.

Role obligations of librarians were analysed in terms of three orientations: inner-directed, organisation-directed and collectively-directed. The majority of librarians derive satisfaction by serving their clients. For such professional users are a source of ego-satisfaction. In contrast, a sizable percentage of librarians perceive their roles in terms of organisational responsibilities. It is important to note that very few librarians perceive their role in terms of collectivity orientation. In other words, role-obligations of a majority of librarians relates to the immediate needs of the clients they interact with rather than the utility of their service for the larger society.

Role image of librarians were investigated in two contexts: (a) their definition of role image and (b) the organisational definition of role image. An overwhelming majority of respondents indicate client orientation in their self-role image. Less than one-fifth of the librarians projected bureaucratic or professional orientations in their self-role image. Self-role image of librarians did not correspond with what they thought was their organisational image. In organisational role image, there is sharp decrease in the client orientation and a substantial increase in bureaucratic orientation. While a majority of librarians (65.5

per cent) project client orientation as their self-role image, only 38 per cent of them consider that client orientation was actually valued in the organisations. In contrast, bureaucratic orientation is much lower in the self-role image but tended to become higher in the organisational context. Thus, there was a clear indication that organisational patterns of libraries, their rules and regulations are not conducive to the advancement of service ideals. If bureaucratic orientation tends to increase, it would certainly minimize the service-ethos. It may also be partly correct to think that the projection of high client orientation held by the majority of librarians in their self-role image may be the result of their low level of professionalisation. On the other hand, low prestige and low level of professionalisation are likely to contribute towards bureaucratic orientation.

VALUE ORIENTATIONS AND ROLE RELATIONS

Value orientations of librarians were examined in order to find out whether there were any other factors in addition to the organisational constraints which are responsible for the erosion of service ideals. The findings indicated that self-role images of librarians are in conformity with their value orientations. Only a small percentage of librarians hold negative attitude towards bureaucratic values whereas the majority of librarians indicate positive values towards professional orientations and client service.

As librarians hold very high positive values towards service ideals we also analysed their perspectives of client service. While more than 50 per cent of librarians indicate a development perspective in clients' service, a sizable number of them also serve their clients with humanitarian motives. However, librarians who hold bureaucratic perspective in regard to client service constitute only a negligible percentage.

In the role-set of librarians three basic types of role relations have been envisaged; superior-subordinate relations, colleaguial, and professional-client relations.

Superior-subordinate relations were studied from two dimensions: bureaucratic and professional. Bureaucratic role relations were examined in relation to the delegation of authority and the sharing of organisational responsibilities by both the superiors and subordinates.

Delegation of authority to the subordinates and superiors' willingness to share responsibilities were examined in case of middle level and junior level professionals. The junior level professionals thought that the superiors were more favourably inclined toward delegation of power as compared with their middle level seniors. However, the extent of delegation of power would depend upon subordinates' willingness to assume responsibility. Respondents in this study clearly indicated that senior librarians were highly committed to the performance of their roles by shouldering a great deal of responsibility. In contrast, less than half of the senior and middle level librarians were of the opinion that their subordinates are willing to take responsibility, if assigned. In this regard it is important to note that one-fourth of professionals in both superior and subordinate categories are unwilling to share any kind of responsibility.

In regard to professional relations with superiors, nearly 60 per cent of junior librarians consider their superiors to be bureaucratic-authoritarian who did not show much concern for the professional development of their juniors. Professional-equalitarian superiors constitute only a negligible percentage.

The distinctive feature of the colleaguial relations is that the majority of respondents maintain informal equalitarian relations in respect of professional and administrative matters with their colleagues. Informal equalitarian relations were more strong in the case of junior librarians and female professionals. But there were at least one-third of the professionals who would not like to interact with their colleagues. Moreover, a sizable group of librarians are suspicious of their colleagues. Undoubtedly both these characteristics — withdrawal and suspicious — are not conducive to the growth of professionalism.

Majority of librarians perform indirect service to the clients. In order to understand the professional-client relations, an attempt was made to unfold the ideal and actual role-images the clients hold of librarians. An overwhelming majority of clients evaluated the ideal role of librarians in terms of client orientation and only a small percentage of the clients considered librarians to be bureaucratically oriented. For the clients, professional role of librarians do not find place in their ideal role image. But the most important finding was that less than half of the clients perceive the librarians as client-oriented in their actual role image. A greater amount of similarity exists between clients' perceptions of actual role attributes of librarians and librarians' perception of organisational role image of themselves. Perceptions of both librarians and clients more or less confirm that organisational values do not lay much stress on service orientation. On the contrary, these values provide support to bureaucratic orientation. However, in organisational context more than one-fourth of the clients were able to recognise professional role of librarians. More than half of them had interaction with the librarians only 'some times', while more than one-fourth of them did not find any opportunity to interact with the librarians. Partly, this is so because the librarians usually fail to project their appropriate role image in organisations.

BUREAUCRATISATION AND PROFESSIONALISATION

For investigating the degree of bureaucratisation, three structural dimensions of bureaucracy, viz., centralisation, specialisation and formalisation were selected. For examining the extent of professionalisation, the following attitudinal components were utilised: (1) commitment to professional orientation, (2) client-orientation and (3) work-related autonomy and utilisation of professional knowledge and skill.

In respect to bureaucratisation we find that library as an organisation does not score high in regard to all dimensions of bureaucracy. Libraries seem to be quite low in respect to specialisation whereas they are high on the dimension of centralisation. The implication is that the absence of specialised roles in libraries is likely to increase the routine activities which need to be supervised or controlled by a hierarchical system.

A higher percentage of women librarians perceive a greater degree of centralisation due to their lack of participation in decision-making process. Perhaps this is due to the fact that they are largely concentrated at the junior level in libraries. Women librarians also perceive higher degree of specialisation due to their relatively more technical nature of roles they are assigned. In contrast, male librarians experience higher degree of formalisation because of their greater involvement in administrative roles.

The process of bureaucratisation does not seem to operate equally in all types of libraries. University and public libraries are found to be highly centralised and formalised as compared to the special libraries. It has also been seen that specialisation does not seem to operate satisfactorily in any type of libraries. Specialisation in public libraries exists at the minimum level.

In respect of professional dimension a large percentage of respondents show high client-orientation, while they are low on the dimensions of autonomy and commitment. Women librarians indicate low level of professionalisation. Higher level of professionalism is found to be closely associated with higher professional ranks. Generally, organisational milieu of librarians does not make much difference in their degree of professionalisation. However, public librarians show slightly lower level of professionalisation.

Professionals in organisations share both professional and bureaucratic values. Hence, the inter-relationship between bureaucratisation and professionalisation was examined. Findings in this regard indicate that bureaucratic ethos prevailing in libraries greatly affects professional commitment. In other words, higher the bureaucratisation, lower the professional commitment. Another professional dimension which is affected by the process of bureaucratisation is autonomy. In this regard we find that lower the bureaucratisation, higher the autonomy. As regards to the third dimension, i.e., client-orientation it seems that professionals are likely to preserve it, irrespective of their organisational milieu.

Both bureaucratisation and professionalisation are inevitable processes for the organisational professionals. However, it is necessary to keep the appropriate balance and mix. In the case of librarianship, it is the bureaucratic dimensions which inhibit the growth of professionalism. Professional autonomy and commitment are seriously eroded by the bureaucratic process. Professionals' claim for high client orientation seems to be anchored to their low level of professionalisation. Clients usually fail to believe that professionals can perform expert-role when needs arise. Even if professionals think that they can perform such a role, they are incapacitated by the bureaucratic structure of their organisations. Librarians have, thus, low professional image due to the lack of role-specificity and weak professional-client relations. Role-diffusion seems to be a major problem for librarians.

Professionalisation suffers from many constraints. Poor material rewards, limited possibility of career mobility, inadequate communication about the ethos of the profession, etc., result in weak pre-entry motivation. Inadequate occupational socialisation and bureaucratic role-structures often fail to develop strong professional commitments and appropriate role images among librarians. Lack of upward mobility, low occupational prestige and bureaucratic authoritarian role-relations create further bottlenecks in the process of professionalisation of librarians.

APPENDIX I

LIBRARIES SELECTED FOR THE SAMPLE

Sl. No.	Name of the Library	Collection	Annual budget in lacs	No. of professional staff
1	2	3	4	5
University Libraries				
1.	All India Institute of Medical Sciences, B.B. Dixit Library, (1956)	49600	10.00	8
2.	Delhi University Library System, (1922)	934036	55.15	93
3.	Indian Agricultural Research Institute Library, (1905)	300000	10.90	12
4.	Indian Institute of Technology Library, (1961)	121030	30.00	23
5.	Jamia Millia Islamia, Dr. Zakir Husain Library, (1920)	170000	1.60	11
Public Libraries				
6.	Central Secretarial Library	700000	27.00	27
7.	Delhi Public Library, (1951)	732606	48.40	24
Special Libraries				
8.	Department of Science and Technology Library	25394	1.40	4
9.	Indian Council of World Affairs, (1943)	110000	1.10	9

(Contd.)

(Contd.)

1	2	3	4	5
10.	Indian Council of Historical Research, (1973)	25000	3.0	4
11.	Indian Institute of Public Administration, (1954)	140000	2.25	11
12.	Indian Standard Institution Technical Library, (1943)	500000	4.20	15
13.	Indian Statistical Institute Library, (1955)	200000	2.00	4
14.	Institute for Defence Studies and Analysis, (1965)	300000	4.5	4
15.	National Council of Applied Economic Research, (1956)	47000	75.00	4
16.	National Council of Educational Research and Training Department of Library and Documentation and Information (NA)	120000	4.8	14
17.	National Institute of Health and Family Welfare, National Documentation Centre, (1970)	30000	5.00	11
18.	National Medical Library, Director-General of Health Services, Govt. of India, (1966)	247000	118.00	13
19.	Nehru Memorial Museum and Library, (1964)	94262	5.0	14
20.	National Physical Laboratory Library, (1950)	91800	11.50	10
21.	National Science Library (INSDOC), (1964)	105000	25.0	15
22.	National Social Science Documentation Centre, ICSSR, (1970)	15000	1.50	25

Notes: The years shown in parentheses indicate the year of establishment.

APPENDIX II

HIERARCHICAL POSITIONS OF PROFESSIONAL LIBRARIANS IN DIFFERENT TYPES OF LIBRARIES

Hierarchical levels	Comparable designation or grade	Pay-Scale according to III Pay Commission of India
I Senior	Librarian	1500 - 2500
		1500 - 2000
	Director	1800 - 2000
		1600 - 2000
	Scientist - E	1500 - 2000
		1300 - 1700
	Deputy Librarian	1200 - 1900
	Dy. Director/Scientist/T.7	1100 - 1600
II Middle	Asstt. Librarian	700 - 1600
	Documentation Officer	700 - 1600
	Asstt. Director/Scientist-	700 - 1300
	B/T.6/T.5	700 - 1300
	Librarian Grade I	650 - 1250
III Junior	Professional Asstt.	550 - 900
	T.4/Documentation Asstt.	550 - 900
	Librarian Grade II/ Sr.Technical Asstt./T.3	425 - 700

APPENDIX III

INDEX OF CENTRALISATION

Centralisation involves the location of decision-making. An organisation is considered to be centralised if most decisions are made at top. If decisions are scattered through units and levels, it is decentralised. Hierarchical differentiation in an organisation interferes with the participation of decision making.

Index of Centralisation was constructed on the basis of the following items. The scores assigned to the responses have been shown in the table below:

Index of Centralisation of Decision Making

Items	Responses	Scores
1. In your library, do you have a chance to take decision, of your own without asking any one higher in your library?	Mostly	1
	Often Sometimes	2
	Seldom	3
2. "There can be little action taken in your library until a superior approves a decision." How accurately does this statement describe the day-to-day work of your library?	Mostly accurate	3
	Largely accurate Fairly accurate	2
	Largely inaccurate Mostly inaccurate	1
3. How much say do you think your superior has in matters that affect you and your work?	A very great deal of say A considerable say	3
	Some say	2
	Little say Not at all	1

The total score varies between 3 to 9. The cut off points were decided as per procedure indicated in Chapter Two. The distribution of the respondents according to the index are: High (47.0 per cent), moderate (25.7 per cent) and low (27.3 per cent).

APPENDIX IV

INDEX OF SPECIALISATION

Specialisation is concerned with the division of labour within the organisation. A formal organisation is also called a complex organisation because roles are highly differentiated, both vertically and horizontally. Complexity is, thus, one of the characteristics of a larger organisation.

The following items were used for creating an Index for Specialisation. Items and the corresponding scores given to the responses have 1been presented in the table below:

Index for Specialisation

Items	Responses	Scores
1. Does your position require you to do similar things which are performed by your immediate superior?	Almost all things	
	Many things	1
	Something	2
	Few things	
	Practically none	3
2. If you are substituting a person to do the work of your present position, do you think that he should have the education and experience that you possess.	Practically all of it	
	A large part of it	3
	Some of it	2
	Little of it	
	Really none of it	1
3. How will you describe the work that you do in your present position? Is it . . . ?	All repetitive	
	Largely repetitive	3
	Somewhat repetitive	2
	Mostly non-repetitive	
	Entirely non-repetitive	1

That total score varies between 3 and 9. The respondents were grouped on the basis of cut-off points as discussed in Chapter Two. The respondents' rating on the Index of Specialisation are: High (21.0 per cent), Moderate (34.0 per cent) and low (45.0 per cent).

APPENDIX V

INDEX OF FORMALISATION

'Formalisation' relates to the use of rules in an organisation. It denotes the extent to which rules, procedures, instructions and communications are written or specified for guiding or regulating the behaviour of the job occupants.

On the basis of the following items on Index of Formalisation was constructed. The scores assigned to the items have been presented in the table below:

Index of Formalisation

Items	Responses	Scores
1. In performing your job, do you feel that there are enough rules and regulations which give you fairly clear indications for handling your work?	Rather excessive More than excessive	3
	Just enough	2
	Little Too little	1
2. Would you agree that most of your day-to-day work consists of the applications of prescribed rules and procedures with little scope for variation of adoption in your functioning?	Entirely agree Largely agree	3
	Somewhat agree	2
	Largely disagree Entirely disagree	1
3. Whether reader is satisfied with me or not it does not bother me so long as I deal with him according to the rules and regulations, how far do you agree with the statement?	Entirely agree Largely agree	3
	Somewhat agree	2
	Largely disagree Entirely disagree	1

The total score varies between 3 and 9. The cut-off points were decided according to procedure mentioned in Chapter Two. The ratings of the respondents on the above Index are: High (46.5 per cent), Moderate (27.0 per cent) and low (26.5 per cent).

APPENDIX VI

INDEX OF WORK AUTONOMY AND UTILISATION OF PROFESSIONAL KNOWLEDGE AND SKILL

In order to examine work autonomy and professional contents in work, an index for the same was constructed with the following items. The scores given to the responses are indicated against the items.

Items	Responses	Scores
1. Do you think that a person in your position is expected to . . . ?	Make his own decisions	3
	Make only minor decision and refer the major ones to the superior	2
	Get guidance from the superior at all the superior at all the times	1
2. Do you think in your present job professional training and academic qualifications are . . . ?	Fully utilised	3
	Moderately utilised	2
	Little utilised	1
3. Does your work require you to devise new ways and means of doing things?	To a great extent To a considerable extent	3
	To some extent	2
	Little Not al all	1

The total score varies between 3 and 9. The cut-off points were decided as indicated in Chapter Two. The respondents' distribution on the scale are: High (31.0 per cent), Moderate (50.5 per cent) and low (18.5 per cent).

APPENDIX VII

CLIENT ORIENTATION INDEX

Based on three questions, a Client-Orientation Index was developed. The following table presents the items and scores given to them:

Items	Responses	Scores
1. "All professionals in the library should directly help the users even if they are placed in different sections or they have been assigned specific work." How far do you agree?	Entirely agree Largely agree	3
	Somewhat agree	2
	Disagree Entirely disagree	1
2. "The professionals in the library should realise that helping the users directly would provide them an opportunity to grow professionally, therefore, they should help the users and try to finish their specific work by some way or other." How far do you agree?	Entirely agree Largely agree	3
	Somewhat agree	2
	Entirely disagree Largely disagree	1

The total score ranges between 2 and 6. The cut-off points were decided as explained in the Chapter Two. The respondents were distributed on the Index in the following manner: High (42.2 per cent), Moderate (37.7 per cent) and Low (20.1 per cent).

BIBLIOGRAPHY

SOCIOLOGY AND OTHER DISCIPLINES

Aiken, M. and Hage, J., (1966). "Organisational Alienation: A Comparative Analysis", *American Sociological Review*, Vol. 31, pp.497-507.

Bali, Arun P., (1986). *College Teachers: Challenges and Response*, New Delhi: Northern Book Centre.

Barker, B., (1963). "Some Problems in the Sociology of Professions", *Daedulus*, Vol. 92, pp.669-88.

Becker, Howard S., (1960). "Notes on the Concept of Commitment", *American Journal of Sociology*, Vol. 66, pp.32-42.

— (1971). *Sociological Work: Methods and Substance*, London: Allen Lane, The Penguin Press.

Ben-David, Joseph, (1958). "Professional Role of the Physicians in Bureaucratised Medicine: A Study in the Role Conflict", *Human Relations*, Vol. 2, pp.901-11.

Bernard, J., (1964). *Academic Women*, Pennsylvania: The Pennsylvania State University Press.

Blau, Peter M., (1956). *Bureaucracy in Modern Society*, New York: Random House, pp.13-25.

— and Duncan, Otis Dundley, (1967). *American Occupational Structure*, New York: John Wiley.

— and Scott, W. Richard, (1970). *Formal Organisation – A Comparative Approach*, London: Routledge and Kegan Paul.

— et al., (1956). "Occupational Choice: A Conceptual Framework", *Industrial and Labour Relations Review*, Vol. 9, pp.266-79.

Bose, Ashish, (1975). "Demographic Profile of Indian Women", in Devaki Jain (ed.), *Indian Women*, New Delhi: Publications Division, Ministry of Information and Broadcasting, 1975.

Bucher, Rue and Stellings, Joan, (1969). "Characteristics of Professional Organisations", *Journal of Health and Social Behaviour*, Vol. 10, pp.3-15.

Caplow, Theodore, (1970). *Sociology of Work*, Allahabad: Central Book Depot, 1970.

Carr-Saunders, A.M., (1955). "Metropolitan Conditions and Traditional Professional Relationships". in Moore Fisher (ed.), *Metropolis in Modern Life*, New York: Doubleday, pp.286-87.

Chitnis, Suma, (1979). "College Teachers: Constraints and Professionalisation", in Suma Chitnis and P.G. Attbach (eds.), *Indian Academic Profession*, Delhi: Macmillan.

Clark, Carroll D. and Gist, Noel P., (1938). "Intelligence as a Factor in Occupational Choice", *American Sociological Review*, Vol. 3, pp.683-94.

Dalton, Melville, (1950). "Conflicts Between Staff and Line Managerial Officers", *American Sociological Review*, Vol. 15, pp.342-51.

Dalton, Melville, (1959). *Men Who Manage*, New York: John Willey.

Daniels, Arlene, K., (1969). "Captive Professional: Bureaucratic Limitations in the Practice of Military Psychiatry", *Journal of Health and Social Behaviour*, Vol. 10, pp.255-65.

Davis, Kingsley, (1949). *Human Society*, New York: Macmillan.

— and Moore, Wilbert E., (1962). "Social Allocation of Occupations: A Functional Analysis", in Sigmund Nosow and William H. Forma (eds.), *Man, Work and Society*, New York: Basic Books.

Dingwall, Robert and Lewis Philip (eds.), (1983). *The Sociology of the Profession: The Lawyers, Doctors and Others*, London: Macmillan.

Driver, Edwin D., (1962). "Caste and Occupational Structure in Central India", *Social Forces*, Vol. 41, pp.26-36.

Dubey, S.M., (1973). *Social Mobility Among the Professions: Study of the Professions in a Transitional Indian Society*, Bombay: Popular Prakashan.

Elliot, Philip, (1972). *Sociology of the Professions*, London: Macmillan.

Etzioni, Amitai, (1964). *Modern Organisation*, Englewood Cliffe, New Jersey: Prentice-Hall.

—, (ed.), (1969). *The Semi-Professions and Their Organisation: Teachers, Nurses and Social Worker*, New York: Free Press.

Flexner, Abraham, (1915). "Is Social Work a Profession?" in *Proceedings of the National Conference on Charities and Corrections*, Chicago: Hildman, pp.576-90.

Froomkin, Joseph and Jaffe, A.J., (1953). "Occupational Skill and Socio-Economic Structure", *American Journal of Sociology*, Vol. 59, pp.42-48.

— , (1982). Sociology of Professions: *Theories and Applications*, New Delhi: (Mimeographed).

Ghurye, G.S., (1961). *Caste, Class and Occupation*, Bombay: Popular Prakashan.

Gist, Noel, (1954). "Caste Differentials in South India", *American Sociological Review*, Vol. 10, pp.130-34.

Glaser, Barney, (1926). "Local Cosmopolitan Scientists", *American Journal of Sociology*, Vol. 69, pp.249-59.

Goffman, Erving, (1972). *Encounters: Two Studies in the Sociology of Interaction*, London: Allen Lane, The Penguin Press.

Goldner, Fred H. and Ritti, R.R., (1967). "Professionalisation as Career Immobility", *American Journal of Sociology*, Vol. 72, pp.489-502.

Goode, William J., (1960). "Encroachment, Charlatanism and the Emerging Profession: Psychology, Sociology and Medicine", *American Sociological Review*, Vol. 25, pp.902-14.

— , (1969). "Theoretical Limits of Professionalisation" in Amitai Etzioni (ed.), *Semi-Professions and Their Organisation: Teachers, Nurses and Social Worker*, New York: Free Press, pp.266-313.

Gore, M.S. et al., (1970). "School Teachers in India: Findings of all India Study in Sociology of Education", in Satya Pal Ruhela (ed.) *Sociology of the Teaching Profession in India*, New Delhi: National Council of Educational Research and Training, pp.83-122.

Greenwood, Ernest, (1957). "Attributes of a Profession", *Social Work*, Vol. 2, pp.44-45.

Gross, Edward, (1958). *Work and Society*, New York: Thomas Y. Crowell.

Gross, M.E.W., (1961). "Influence and Authority Among Physicians in an Out-patient Clinic", *American Sociological Review*, Vol. 26, pp.39-50.

Hage, Jerald and Aiken, Michael (1968). "Relationship of Centralisation to other Structural Properties", *Administrative Science Quarterly*, Vol. 12, pp.72-92.

Hall, Oswald, (1948). "Stages of a Medical Career", *American Journal of Sociology*, Vol. 53, pp.327-36.

Hall, Richard H., (1963). "Concept of Bureaucracy", *American Journal of Sociology*, Vol. 59, pp.32-40.

—— , (1961). *Occupations and Social Structure*, Englewood Cliffs, New Jersey: Prentice-Hall.

—— , (1968). "Professionalisation and Bureaucratisation", *American Sociological Review*, Vol. 33, pp.92-103.

—— , (1967). "Some Organisational Considerations in the Professional Organisational Relationship", *Administrative Science Quarterly*, Vol. 12, pp.461-78.

—— and Tittle, Charles R., (1966-67). "Note on Bureaucracy and its Correlates". *American Journal of Sociology*, Vol. 72, pp.267-72.

Harries-Jankins, G., (1970). "Professionals in Organisations", in J.A. Jackson (ed.), *Professions and Professionalisation*, London: Cambridge University Press.

Hatt, Paul K. and North, C.C., (1962). "Prestige Ratings of Occupations", in Sigmund Nosow and William H. Form (eds.), *Man, Work and Society*, New York: Basic Books.

Hickson, David J., (1965). "Convergence in Organisational Theory", *Administrative Science Quarterly*, Vol. 11, p.225.

Hodge, Robert W. et al., (1966). "Comparative Study of Occupational Prestige", in Reinhard Bendix and S.M. Lipset (eds.), *Class, Status and Power*, New York: Free Press, pp.309-21.

—— et al., (1964). "Occupational Prestige in the United States 1925-63", *American Journal of Sociology*, Vol. 70, pp.286-302.

Hughes, E.C., (1958). *Men and Their Work*. Glencoe, Ill.: Free Press, 1958.

—— , (1960). "Professions in Society", *Canadian Journal of Economics and Political Science*, Vol. 26, pp.54-61.

—— , (1963). "Professions", *Daedalus*, Vol. 92, pp.655-68.

Hunks, Gardner and Schmidt, C. James, (1975). "Alternative Model of a Profession for Librarian", *College and Research Libraries*, Vol. 36, pp.175-87.

India, Status of Women in India (Committee on-), (1971). *Report: Towards Equality*, New Delhi: Ministry of Education and Social Welfare.

India, University Education Commission (December 1948 – August 1949). *Report*.

Jackson, J.A. (ed.), (1970). *Professions and Professionalisation*, London: Cambridge University Press.

—— , (1972). *Role*, London Cambridge University Press.

Jain, Kagzi, Mangal Chandra, (1984). *Constitution of India*, 2 Vols. Vol. 1, 4th ed., Delhi: Metropolitan Book Co.

Jeffrey, St. Clair and Rao, Aluri, (1977). "Staffing the Reference Desk: Professional or Non-Professionals", *Journal of Academic Administration*, Vol. 3, pp.149-53.

Johnson, Malcolm, (1983). "Professional Careers and Biographies", in Robert Dingwall and Philip Lewis (eds.), *Sociology of the Profession: The Lawyers, Doctors and Others*, London: Macmillan, p.21.

Johnson, Terenee J., (1972). *Professions and Power*, London: Macmillan.

Khanna, Kirti, (1987). *Role Structure of Academics: A Profile of Jodhpur University Teachers*, Jodhpur: Jain Brothers.

Kornhauser, W. (1967). *Scientists in Industry: Conflict and Accommodation*, Berkley: University of California Press.

Lambert, R.D., (1963). *Workers, Factories and Social Change in India*, Princeton: Asia Publishing House and Gokhale Institute of Politics and Economics.

Laski, Harold J., (1935). "Decline of the Profession", *Harper's Monthly Magazine*, November, pp.656-57.

Lenski, G. (1966). *Power and Privilege*, New York; McGraw-Hill.

Linton, Ralph, (1936). *Study of Man*, New York: D Appleton-Century.

Lipset, S.M. and Bendix, R. (1959). *Social Mobility in Industrial Society*, Berkley: University of California Press.

Litwak, Eugene, (1961). "Models of Bureaucracy which Permit Conflict", *American Journal of Sociology*, Vol. 67, pp.177-84.

Madan, T.N., (1972). "Doctors in a North Indian City: Recruitment, Role Perception and Role Performance", in S.C. Dube (ed.), *Transactions of the Indian Institute of Advanced Study*, Simla, pp.77-110.

——, (1980). "India: Doctors at the All India Institute of Medical Sciences", in T.N. Madan et al., *Doctors and Society: Three Asian Case Studies, India, Malaysia and Sri Lanka*, Gaziabad: Vikas, p.8.

Marshall, T.H., (1939). "Recent History of Professionalism in Relation to Social Structure and Social Policy", *Canadian Journal of Economics and Political Science*, Vol. 5, pp.337-38.

Merton, Robert K., (1952). "Bureaucratic Structure and Personality", in *Reader in Bureaucracy*, Glencoe, Ill.: Free Press, pp.361-71.

——, (1957). *Social Theory and Social Structure*, Rev. ed. New York: Free Press.

Miller, Dilbert C. and Form, William H., (1951). *Industrial Sociology*, New York: Harper.

Montagna, Paul D., (1968). "Professionalisation and Bureaucratisation in Large Professional Organisation", *American Journal of Sociology*, Vol. 74, pp.138-45.

—— , (1977). *Occupation and Society: Towards a Sociology of the Labour Market*, London: John Wiley.

Moore, Wilbert E., (1970). *Professions: Role and Rule*, New York: Russel Sage Foundation, 1970.

Moser, C.A. and Hall, J.R., (1954). "Social Grading of Occupations", in D.A.V. Glass (ed.), *Social Mobility in Britain*, London: Routledge and Kegan Paul, 1954.

Mowday, Richard, et al., (1982). *Employee-Organisation Linkages: The Psychology of Commitment, Absentism and Turnover*, New York: Academic Press.

Nosow, Sigmund and Form, William H., (eds.), (1962). *Man, Work and Society*, New York: Basic Books.

Nyrop, Richard F. et al., (1957). *Area Handbook for India*, Washington D.C.: American University.

Oommen, T.K., (1978). *Doctors and Nurses: A Study of Occupational Role Structure*, Delhi: Macmillan.

—— , (1983). "Legal Profession in India: Some Sociological Perspectives", *Indian Bar Review*, Vol. 10, pp.1-46.

Pai Panandiker, V.A. and Kshirsagar, S.S., (1978). *Bureaucracy and Development Administration*, New Delhi: Centre for Policy Research.

Parker, Ralph H., (1962). "Ports of Entry to Librarianship", in Philip H. Ennis, and Howard W. Winger (eds.), *Seven Questions About the Profession of Librarianship*, Chicago, Illinois: University of Chicago Press.

Parsons, Talcott, (1954). *Essays in Sociological Theory*, Glencoe, Illinois: Free Press.

—— , (1951). *Social System*, Glencoe, Ill.: Free Press, pp.38-39.

Pugh, D.S. et al., "Dimensions of Organisation Structure", *Administrative Science Quarterly*, Vol. 13, 1968, pp.65-105.

Reiss, Albert J., Jr. et al., (1961). *Occupations and Social Status*, New York: Free Press.

Reynolds, Lloyd G., (1951). *Structure of Labour Markets*, New York: Harper.

Riessman, Leonard, (1949). "Study of Role Conceptions in Bureaucracy", *Social Forces*, Vol. 27, pp. 305-10.

Ritzer, George, (1972). *Man and His Work*, New York: Appleton-Century Crofts.

Robinson, John P. et al., (1969). *Measures of Occupational Characteristics*, Ann Arbor, Michigan: University of Michigan Survey Research Centre, Institute for Social Research.

Rosenberg, M. et al., (1957). *Occupations and Values*, Glencoe, Ill.: Free Press, 1957.

Roth, Jullius A., (1974). "Professionalism: Sociologist Decoy", *Sociology of Work and Occupations*, Vol. 1, pp.6-23.

Ruhela, Satya Pal, (1980). "Professionalisation of School Teachers in India", National Seminar of the Sociology of the Professions (October 13-16, 1984), The University of Jodhpur, Department of Sociology, Jodhpur (Mimeographed).

Scott, W. Richard, (1966). "Professionals in Bureaucracies: Areas of Conflict", in Howard M. Vollumer and Donald M. Mills (eds.), *Professionalisation*, Englewood Cliffs, Prentice-Hall, pp.265-75.

—, (1965). "Reactions to Supervision in a Heteronomous Professional Organisation", *Administrative Science Quarterly*, Vol. 10, pp.67-81.

Sharma, K.L., (1984). *Sociology of Law and Legal Professions*, Jaipur: Rawat.

Sharma, S.L., (1985). "Sociology of Professions in India", in *Survey of Research in Sociology and Social Anthropology, 1969-1979* (Vol. 2) (A Project Sponsored by the Indian Council of Social Science Research, New Delhi: Satvahan).

Simpson, Richard L. and Simpson, Ida Harper, (1960-61). "Values, Personal Influence and Occupational Choice", *Social Forces*, Vol. 39, pp.116-25.

— , (1969). "Women and Bureaucracy in the Semi Professions", in Amitai Etzioni (ed.), *Semi-Professions and Their Organisations*, London: Free Press, pp.196-247.

Slater, Margaret, (1979). *Career Patterns and the Occupational Choice*, London: ASLIB (Occasional Publication No. 23).

Smigel, Erwin, (1969). *Wall Street Lawyer*, Bloomington: Indiana University Press.

Solcum, W.C., (1966). *Occupational Careers*, Chicago: Aldine.

Soloman, David N., (1968). "Sociological Perspectives on occupations", in Howard S. Becker, et al., *Institutes and the Persons*, Chicago: Aldine, pp.3-13

Srinivas, M.N., (1962) *Caste in Modern India*, Bombay: Asia Publishing House.

Steers, R.M., (1977). "Antecedents of Outcomes of Organisational Commitment", *Administrative Science Quarterly*, Vol. 22, pp.46-56.

Strong, Edward K., (1935). "Predictive Value of the Vocational Interest Test", *Journal of Educational Psychology*, Vol. 26, pp.331-49.

Super, Donald E. and Wright, R., (1940). "From School of Work in the Depression Years", *School Review*, Vol. 49, pp.120-30.

Tausky, Curt, (1983). "Formal Organisation", in Robert Hagedom, *Sociology*, Dubuque, Iowa: Wm. C. Brown.

Thomas, Edwin J. and Biddle, Bruce J., (1966). "Nature and History or Role Theory", in Bruce J. Biddle and Edwin J. Thomas (eds.), *Role Theory: Concepts and Research*, New York: John Wiley.

Thompson, james D., et al., (1962). *Occupations: Personnel and Careers*, Pittsburgh: University of Pittsburgh, pp.12-14.

Tumin, Melvin M., (1953). "Some Principles of Stratification: A Critical Analysis", *American Sociological Review*, Vol. 18, pp.287-95.

Turner, C. and Hodge, M.N., (1970). "Occupations and Professions", in J.A. Jackson (ed.), *Professions and Professionalisation*, London: Cambridge University Press.

Udy, Stanley H. Jr., (1959). "Bureaucracy and Rationality in Weber's Organisation Theory: An Empirical Study", *American Sociological Review*, Vol. 24, pp.791-795.

University Grants Commission (India), (1985). *Facilities to Scheduled Castes and Scheduled Tribes in University and Colleges* (Analysis on the Position of Actual Admissions and Employment of Scheduled Castes and Scheduled Tribes in Universities and Colleges during 1978-79), New Delhi: U.G.C.

Vollumer, Howard M. and Mills, Donald L. (ed.), (1966). *Professionalisation*, Englewood Cliffs, New Jersey: Prentice-Hall.

Weber, Max, (1946). *From Max Weber: Essays in Sociology*, (ed.), Hans H. Gerth and C. Wright Mills, London: Oxford University Press.

—— , (1947). *Theory of Social and Economic Organisation*, translated by A.M. Hendrson and Talcott Parsons, New York: Oxford University Press.

Wilensky, H.L., (1964). "Professionalisation of Every One", *American Journal of Sociology*, Vol. 70, pp.137-58.

Wilensky, Harold J., (1962). "Careers, Life Styles and Social Integration" in Sigmond Nosow and William H. Form (eds.), *Man, Work and Society*, New York: Basic Books.

—— , (1960). "Work, Careers and Social Interaction", *International Social Science Journal*, Vol. 12, pp.543-560.

Wilson, Everett K., (1966). *Sociology: Rules, Roles and Relationships*, Homeland, Illinois: Dorsey Press.

Yogendra Singh, (1979). "Academic Role Structure and Modernisation: A Study of Rajasthan University Teachers", in Suma Chitnis and Philip G. Althach (eds.), *Indian Academic Profession*, Delhi: Macmillan.

LIBRARY SCIENCE LITERATURE

Anand, A.K. et al., (1987). "Career Opportunities and Prospects for Library and Information Science Personnel in India", *IASLIC Bulletin*, Vol. 27, pp.77-92.

Anand, J.K., (1983). "Academic Status of University and College Librarians in India: A Retrospective Study", in P.B. Mangla et al. (ed.), *Fifty Years of Librarianship in India: Past, Present and Future* (Seminar Papers of Twenty Ninth All India Library Conference, Mysore University, December 5-9, 1983), Delhi: Indian Library Association.

Bhardwaj, B.L., (1986). "Library Associations of India", in B.M. Gupta et al., (eds.), *Handbook of Libraries Archives and Information Centres in India*, Vol. 2, New Delhi: Information Industry Publications, pp.755-66.

Biggs, Mary, (1982). "Librarians and the Woman Questions: An Inquiry into the Conservatism", *Journal of Library History*, Vol. 17, pp.409-28.

Birdsall, William F., (1980). "Librarians and Professionalism: Status Measured by Outmoded Models", *Canadian Library Journal*, Vol. 37, pp.145-48.

Bundy, Mary Lee and Wasserman, Paul, (1968). "Professionalism Reconsidered", *College and Research Libraries*, Vol. 29(8), 1968, pp.5-26.

Butler, Pierce, (1931). *Introduction to Library Science*, Chicago: University of Chicago Press.

—— , (1951), "Librarianship as a Profession", *Library Quarterly*, Vol. 21, 1951, pp.235-47.

Chapman, L., (1980). "Popular Images", *New Library World*, Vol. 81, pp.153-54.

Chopra, Hans Raj, (1984). "Librarians' Attitude towards Profession of Librarianship in India: A Study", National Seminar of the Sociology of the Profession (October 13-18, 1984), The University of Jodhpur, Department of Sociology, Jodhpur (mimeographed).

Datta, N., (1985). *Academic Status for Universities and College Libraries in India*, Delhi: Indian Bibliographies.

Derr, Richard, L., (1983). "Interaction of Theory and Practice in Professional Programmes", *Journal of Education for Librarianship*, Vol. 23, pp.193-208.

Depew, John N., (1983). "ACRL Standards for Faculty Status: Panacea or Placebo", *College and Research Libraries*, Vol. 44, pp. 407-20.

Devarajan, G., (1963). "Admission Seeking Variables in Library and Information Science Studies: A Socio-Economic Profile", *ALIS Bulletin*, Vol. 17, pp.37-41.

Directory of Special and Research Libraries in India, (1985). Calcutta: Indian Association of Special Libraries and Information Centres.

Dollard, Peter, (1977). "Look the Loonies in a Stereotype 1", *Library Journal*, Vol. 102 (September 1), pp.1724-25.

Engel, Gloria V., (1970). "Professional Autonomy and Bureaucratic Organisation", *Administrative Science Quarterly*, Vol. 15, pp.12-21.

Flanagan, L.N., (1978). "Enemy Within, the Enemy Without: Two Major Impediments to the Development of Librarianship as a Profession", *Cath, Library World*, Vol. 50, pp.171-76.

Gillis, R., (1976). "Has Librarianship Really Emerged as a Profession?" *Assistant Librarian*, Vol. 69, pp.30-33.

Girja Kumar, (1976). "Academic Status for University and College Libraries", *ILA Bulletin*, Vol. 12, pp.5-14.

—— , (1985). (Thirtieth All India Library Conference, Jaipur, January 28-31, 1985, Presidential Address), Delhi: Indian Library Association.

Girja Kumar and Krishan Kumar, (1983) *Philosophy of User Education*, Delhi: Vikas.

—— , (1962). "Librarian: From Occupation to Profession", in Philip H. Ennis and Howard W. Winger (eds.), *Seven Questions About the Profession of Librarianship*, Chicago: University of Chicago Press, pp.8-22.

Gopinath, M.S., (1967). "Library Profession and Its Evolution", *Library Science with a Slant to Documentation*, Vol. 4, pp.26-2-82.

Gupta, B.M. et al. (eds.), (1986). *Handbook of Libraries, Archieves and Information Centres in India*, Vol. 3, New Delhi: Information Industry Publications.

Gupta, S., (1987). "Library Science as a Career", *Employment News*, Vol. 12, Saturday, 2 May, pp.1-2.

Harrison, K.C., (1970). *Library and the Community*, London: Andre Deutsch, 1977.

Indian Library Directory, (1985). 4th ed., Delhi: Indian Library Association.

Isaac, K.A., (1983). "Development of University Library in India", in P.B. Mangla et al. (eds.), *Fifty years of Librarianship in India: Past, Present and Future* (Seminar Papers of Twenty Ninth All India Library Conference, Mysore University, December 5-9, 1983), Delhi: Indian Library Association.

Kaula, P.N., (1986). "Contributions of Ranganathan and World Librarianship", in T.S. Rajagopalan (ed.), *Ranganathan's Philosophy: Assessment, Impact and Relevance*, Delhi: Vikas.

—— , (1985), *Library Movement in India*, Delhi: Delhi Library Association.

Kumar, P.S.G., (1987). Computerisation of Indian Libraries, Delhi: B.R. Publishing.

Lancour, H., (1962). "Librarians' Search for Status", in Phillip H. Ennis and Howard W. Winger (eds.), *Seven Questions About the Profession of Librarianship*, Chicago: University of Chicago Press, pp.71-83.

Mangla, P.B., (1984-85). "Library and Information Science Education in India", in B.M. Gupta, et al. (eds.), *Handbook of Libraries Archives and Information Centres in India* Vol. 1, New Delhi: Information Industry Publication, pp.229-256.

—— , (1983). et al., *Fifty Years of Librarianship in India: Past, Present and Future* (Seminar Papers of Twenty Ninth All India Library

Conference, Mysore University, December 5-9, 1983), Delhi: Indian Library Association.

Martell, Charles R., (1984). "Myths, Schooling and the Practice of Librarianship", *College and Research Libraries*, Vol. 45(5), pp.374-82.

McGarry, Kevin, (1983). "Education for Librarianship and Information Science: A Retrospect and a Revolution", *Journal of Documentation*. Vol. 49 (2), pp.95-122.

McPherson, Judith, (1974). "Peacocks and Posers– Librarianship as a Profession", *Assistant Librarian*, Vol. 67, p.117.

Mishra, Jogesh, (1979). *History of Libraries and Librarianship Since 1850*, Atma Ram, (1979).

Mukherjee, A.K., *Fundamental of Special Librarianship and Documentation*, Calcutta: IASLIC, 1969.

National Convention of University and College Librarians (New Delhi), (1985). *Faculty Status for University of College Librarianship India: Basic Documents*, New Delhi.

Nayar, B.K. et al., "Demand for Information Scientists in India (an Analysis of Advertised Vacancies)", in B.M. Gupta et al. (eds.), *Handbook of Libraries, Archieves and Information Centres in India*, New Delhi. Information Industry Publications, 1984-85.

Rajagopalan, T.S. (ed.), (1986). *Ranganathan's Philosophy: Assessment, Impact and Relevance*, Delhi: Vikas.

Ranganathan, S.R., (1948). *Preface to Library Science*, Delhi: University of Delhi.

—, (1965). "Status of Library Personnel in India", *Library Herald*, Vol. 8, pp.65-66.

Schiller, Anita R., (1974). "Women in Librarianship", in Melvin J. Voigt (ed.), *Advances in Librarianship*, New York: Academic Press, pp.104-47.

Schwartz, Norda L., (1977). "Professional Attitude", *Library Journal*, Vol. 102, September 1, pp.1729-31.

Schwarzweller, Harry K., (2960-61). "Values and Occupational Choice", *Social Forces*, Vol.39, pp.126-35.

Sergean, R., (1977). *Librarianship and Information Work: Job Characteristics and Staffing Needs*, London: British Library Research and Development Deptt.

Shaffer, Dale Eugene, (1968). *Maturity of Librarianship as a Profession*, Metuchen, New Jersey: Scarecrow Press.

Sharma, Jagdish Saran, (1986). *Library Movement in India and Abroad* New Delhi: E Publications.

Slater, Margaret, (1978). "Career Patterns and Mobility in the Library Information Field", *Aslib Proceedings*, Vol. 30, pp.344-51.

Stockers, R.B., (1976). "Jack of All Trades but Master of What?" *Wilson Library Bulletin*, Vol. 61, pp.326-32.

Thompson, James, (1977). *History of Principles of Librarianship*, London: Clive Bingley.

—— , (1965). *Library Science in Indian Universities: Report of the University Grants Commission Review Committee*, New Delhi: UGC.

——, (1959-60). *Report for the Year* 1959-60.

Williams, G.W. and Woods, A.J., (1964). "Image of the Librarians", *New Library World*, Vol. 75, pp.168-70.

Wilson, Pauline, (1978). "Impending Change in Library Education: Implications for Planning", *Journal of Education for Librarianship*, Vol. 18, pp.159-74.

—— , (1979). "Librarians as Teachers: The Study of an Organisation Fiction", *Library Quarterly*, Vol. 49, pp.146-52.

Wilson, Pauline, (1978). "Librarianship and ALA in a Post-Industrial Society", *American Libraries*, Vol. 9, pp.124-28.

Winger, Howard W., (1964). "Aspects in Librarianship: A Trace Work of History". in Philip H. Ennis and Howard W. Winger (eds.), *Seven Questions About the Profession of Librarianship*, Chicago: University of Chicago, pp.23-37.

Yerkey, A. Neil, (1981). "Psychological Climate of Librarianship: Values of Special Librarians", *Special Libraries*, Vol. 72, pp.195-200.

INDEX